Motorcycle T 

for

Virgins

Simon Bradley

Panther Publishing

Published by Panther Publishing Ltd in 2008
Panther Publishing Ltd
10 Lime Avenue
High Wycombe
Bucks HP11 1DP UK
http://www.panther-publishing.com

Acknowledgements
Thanks to Dalia and Laura for their support; Rapid Tracks
and others for the opportunity to photograph their
sessions; Dave at Brands Hatch, and Rollo at Panther
Publishing for his patience and guidance. And of course
everyone else who helped, knowingly or otherwise....

ISBN 978-0-9556595-0-8

Contents

Introduction

This book is intended as an introduction to track days. It is not intended to be a definitive circuit guide or a manual on how to ride fast. There are plenty of far better books available that deal with those areas, like Keith Code's excellent *Twist of the wrist* for techniques. Instead, this book is aimed at the less experienced trackday rider and attempts to steer them down a path which will maximise their enjoyment and, hopefully, answer at least most of the concerns they will be feeling. I can't give a list of all the trackday organisers as they change quite often, but those of whom I have some experience or knowledge are listed at the back (see page 124). One who I'm confident will be around for a while is Rapid Tracks – a bunch of friendly, supportive bike nuts who happen to be policemen in their day jobs and provide road training as well.

History

How many times has the subject of your bike's performance come up in conversation, especially with non-bikers, only to have them shaking their heads and dismissing its remarkable abilities and value with a simple statement? "But the speed limit is seventy." Or, more telling, "But you can't possibly use that sort of performance on the road..." The trouble is, they've actually got a point, and we all know it. I mean, when you've got the latest and greatest race replica you can easily end up in jail – or worse – just by using its full potential in the first couple of gears. Even the most prosaic of modern bikes will comfortably break the speed limit as well as demolishing all but the most expensive supercars in a straight drag off the lights.

Now there's no way that we are going to break our addiction to bikes which are faster and better handling than we will ever be able to exploit. It's embedded in our national motorcycling psyche, something which is an intrinsic part of the bike scene in the UK. And with the increasingly draconian measures we are seeing used to enforce speed limits, which themselves are being reduced, seemingly arbitrarily, across the country, we need an outlet.

Happily, some time in the mid eighties the idea of renting racetracks out for the four days a week that they weren't doing anything started to gain popularity, both with the circuit owners who saw a way of covering some more of their fixed costs and with riders who saw a way of either emulating their heroes on track or simply letting off steam and having a lot of fun. Trackday companies appeared overnight, arranging public sessions on circuits across the land with varying degrees of professionalism. And an industry was born.

Since then things have got a little more organised. Self regulation has meant that most of the real cowboys have gone and the chances are that any company you book a trackday with now will be more than capable of organising a seriously good day for you.

Preparation

Trackdays are among the best fun that it's possible to have while clothed. Some people reckon that qualifier is misplaced, but I think they should get out more. Or maybe stay in more. Either way, trackdays are an absolute blast. But like many sporting pursuits, you need a little preparation to make sure you have the best time and that all you come away with is well scrubbed tyres and happy memories.

Preparing your bike

If you're a responsible sort, and I'm sure you are, then you regularly check your bike over for safety and roadworthiness anyway. In which case the bike preparation part of getting ready for a track day will be a breeze. We will be discussing scrutineering later under rules and regulations (see p13), so here we'll be looking at what you will need to do to get your bike past the scrutineer's eagle-eye and out onto the track. There are some things which are – or should – be very obvious, as well as a few things that may surprise you.

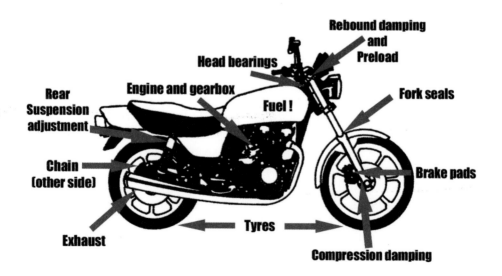

Make sure you check all these before going on the track

Tyres

Tyres don't necessarily have to be road legal because you're not riding on the road. Obviously you need to be legal if you rode to the circuit and, as trackdays can be quite hard on tyres, if you're riding home again you need to be sure there's enough meat on your tyres to still be legal when you leave. But some organisers are happy with slicks (or wets if it's that sort of day) so it isn't an issue if you've got "Not for road use" stamped on the side of your tyres. If you do have road tyres which are worn beyond legal

They're all that keep you from stress testing your leathers and helmet. These are nicely scrubbed in and ready for trackday action...

limits, though, then you will need to persuade the scrutineers that they're safe. It's generally easier to get new ones. One thing you do need to check, regardless, is that your tyres are in good overall condition, free of splits, bulges or screws sticking into them. And make sure they are the right tyre for the bike. And on the right way round – bike tyres are directional and they just don't work properly if the muppet at your local quick fitter has put them on back to front. Don't laugh – I've seen it plenty of times, especially when the customer has brought in loose wheels so there's nothing to check against other than common sense and experience. If you're already an experienced trackday goer you'll have your own tyre pressure preferences, otherwise make sure that the tyres are at the manufacturer's recommended pressures. You'll have plenty of time to fiddle as you get faster, but this gives you a safe basis to work against.

Brake pads, seals and wheel bearings

While you're checking your tyres over, take the opportunity to look at your brake pads. You'll be going faster than usual, hopefully, and will probably be working your brakes harder. So make sure there's plenty of pad material left, because you can bet the scrutineers won't miss it if they're looking marginal. Take a moment to check your brake lines as well, just to make sure they aren't bulging or weeping anywhere, and make sure there's enough fluid in the reservoirs.

Front brake caliper (left of centre) and fork seals (centre top) on a typical sports bike with "upside down" forks. You can see the brake pads if you look into the back (left in this shot) of the caliper.

Less overtly sporty bikes will still have conventional forks like this. The fork seals are at the top of the dull metal sliders, protected by black plastic guards in this case.

While you're on your knees, check that the fork seals aren't leaking (look for an oily deposit on the stanchions where they disappear inside the tubes) and have a waggle on the front and rear wheels to make sure the bearings are OK.

Head bearings

Standing up at the front, and with the bike on the centre stand and someone pushing down on the rear end so the front is off the ground, move the bars from side to side, checking that movement is smooth and that the bars are straight. The giveaway is when you trap one thumb against the tank at full lock, while it's clear on the other side. Also check that the handlebar grips are on securely. If you can get the front wheel off the ground then try to waggle the forks backwards and forwards to make sure the head bearings are OK. Double check that you have full, free and smooth movement lock to lock.

The steering head bearings are under the shiny cap below those two slotted nuts. If you (or a previous owner) are especially prone to wheelying then they may well be, at best, in need of adjustment...

Chain tension

At the back, make sure that chain tension is set according to the manual. A too tight chain will, or could, stop your suspension working properly as it will interfere with the full travel of the back wheel. That will, ultimately, wreck the gearbox sprocket bearing, hugely increase wear on your chain and sprockets and probably kill the cush rubbers in your back wheel. Until then, it'll just muck up the handling. Or at least stop it being as good as it could be. It's also considered bad form to roll up with a chain that's as dry as a warm wind in the Kalahari. Lubing it properly and regularly will make it last longer and make your gearchanges smoother. Your chain gets warm in regular use, and distinctly warm under hard use. Unlubricated chains get bloody hot and have been known to break in extremis. A broken chain is an extremely exciting event for the rider, and really not something you want to experience for the want of a couple of minutes' attention.

Clean, lubed and properly adjusted, this chain is the most efficient transmitter of power you'll find anywhere. The adjusters are just to the left of the wheel spindle in this shot (in front for real)

Suspension

Once you've done the chain, bounce the back up and down a few times to make sure everything moves properly. If you've got twin shocks, make sure they're adjusted the same on each side. Yes, it really does make a difference to the handling!

Engine

Time to take a look at the engine now. Have a quick look over it for leaks, either oil or coolant. Is it running OK? A track day will exacerbate any mechanical problems you may be having, so best get them sorted now. If your bike is due a service then try to get it done a few days beforehand to make sure that you have time to spot and fix any little dealer induced quirks.

Exhaust

While we're looking at the engine, be honest about the exhaust. Does it have a CE or BS mark on it? Is it stamped "Not for road use" or similar? Does it make your ears bleed at 300 paces? If it's louder than is really road legal then you need to be absolutely certain you're going to a noisy day, otherwise the scrutineers will noise test and exclude you.

Suspension adjustment

There's one more thing to look at, but to be honest I can only skim over it here as we could genuinely devote a whole chapter to it. Modern bikes have an enormous amount of suspension adjustment. Some are better than others – some you can twiddle away all day and notice approximately no difference whatsoever, while others give you the ability to completely wreck your bike's handling with a couple of ill considered turns of a screwdriver. Apart from the obvious thing of making sure that both your forks are adjusted the same and also your rear shocks, unless you really know what you're doing, or have the ready advice of a similarly blessed mate, I'd urge you to start off with the suspension set as the designer intended. At least if you do need to make adjustments you'll know where you're starting from...

That's the specifics, so all that remains is a general check-over, basically to make sure that nothing is going to drop off or otherwise cause a hazard. Why not give the bike a clean while you're at it? After all, there will almost certainly be photographers there so you may as well look as good as possible...

Preparing yourself

The best sorted, cleanest bike in the paddock is a great thing to have. But as any racer will tell you, the critical thing is the nut holding the bars. That's you. If your head is in the wrong place, if you're feeling uncomfortable, below par or distracted then you'll not be riding properly and the whole thing becomes a chore instead of a laugh. Of course that's obvious and you already know it. But what can you do about it?

If you're having to steal the time to go, whether from work or spouse, make sure that it's not going to be praying on your mind. A guilty conscience really takes the edge off what you're concentrating on. If you're feeling unwell, or if your prescription medication makes you drowsy then I'd earnestly suggest crying off if you can. Maybe when you book you could get a mate who could step in to fill your slot if you're not able to go. Especially if you have something like hay fever which can flare up and knock you sideways at short notice.

If you're travelling a long way to the circuit then it may well be worth booking yourself into a convenient hotel or B&B. Hardly surprisingly, there are quite a lot to be found around circuits so you shouldn't have to look too hard. Arriving at the circuit for an eight o'clock start after a three hour ride to get there in the first place isn't exactly ideal, especially bearing in mind that you've got the same ride home afterwards...

There are two real problems I usually see people bring with them to trackdays. Of these, by far the most common is fear, or at least trepidation. Now if you're reading this then I'm guessing you're probably not very experienced at track days. That's OK – nobody starts off experienced. But the unknown or unfamiliar can be scary. That's OK too, a bit of anxiety pushes up the adrenaline, makes us more alert and actually makes us ride better. Too much, though, makes us tense and dulls our edge to the point where we no longer function properly. Which is a bad thing. New track day riders bring a load of baggage with them. Funnily enough, if they are honest then the biggest fear isn't falling off and hurting themselves. No, it's looking (or, more accurately, feeling) silly and/or slow. And that's a bit of a problem. Because unless they are blessed with scary amounts of natural talent, in which case they won't be nervous anyway because they'll know, new trackday riders *are* slow. What do you expect? Take someone who's never been on a track before and they are hardly likely to set the lap record, are they? But if they've been honest with the organisers, and the organisers are vaguely competent, then they'll be in a group with other riders who also feel slow. Ultimately, the only person you need to beat is yourself. So just relax, set yourself realistic objectives and have fun. If you've gone with one of the better organisers then you may well have a chance to snag a session with an instructor. Take the opportunity, because it's worth more than I can ever explain in terms of confidence and simple understanding of what you and your bike really can do.

But ultimately, if you're slower than everyone else and still have a laugh, well who really cares? Next time you'll be more relaxed, because you've had fun, you won't be a trackday virgin any more and you'll be quicker than that pasty and shaking first timer.

The other problem people bring with them is actually far harder to deal with. For some reason, if folk travel far enough to a trackday that they need to stay overnight then they seem to think it's mandatory to get completely lashed. I don't know if it's some compensatory thing or what, but it's ever so common. And it means that they get to the track the next day with a hangover or, worse still, over the limit. Being hungover dulls your reactions and concentration and makes you slow and inconsistent. Being over the limit makes you downright dangerous. The scrutineers will invariably spot it if you're unfit to ride and they'll either keep you off the track until you're better or, if you're really unlucky or stupid, nick you for riding under the influence. So here's a simple piece of advice. Have fun, have a drink but don't overdo it. It's just not worth it.

Trackday organisers

It quickly became apparent that trackdays were an exciting business opportunity, and lots of companies sprang up overnight to take advantage of that. Some, perhaps even most, were out to give the best service that they could while a few were out to make a fast buck. Happily most, if not all of the latter have fallen by the wayside and in these enlightened times you can be reasonably confident that whichever company you contact for your trackday will be a professional organisation with a reasonable, um, track record. Sorry.

Different sorts of trackday companies

They may all have their customers' best interests at heart, but trackday companies often go about this in rather different ways. The biggest difference is in the type of rider that they are trying to attract as a customer. Some companies will be aiming their services at the serious trackday goer, while others are more interested in the casual track rider. Some companies even have a customer base made mainly of racers after some extra practice and setup time. It's worth taking the opportunity to find out what sort of company you're talking to before booking, and there are some key things to look for. Probably the most important thing to establish is the company policy regarding groups. You're looking for three groups called something along the lines of novice, intermediate and advanced (or experienced). Remember that's relating to track, not road, experience. You also need the facility to move between groups if necessary. What you really don't want, and I'm assuming that you're not a track veteran here, is a company offering an open pit lane. I'll explain why in a bit.

If you get to talk with someone at the company, then have a careful listen to what they have to say and make sure that you answer their questions honestly. Their response will tell you lots, especially when you mention that this is your first trackday. If you don't get to talk with anyone then you're probably booking online. Have a look at their website and see if you can get an idea of what their main thrust is. Some companies are more angled towards the 'going as fast as you can and getting your knee down approach', while others are more biased towards training you to be quicker and safer, while learning what your bike can do. Both have their place, and which you decide to go for is really entirely up to you. (There is a list of Trackday Companies on page 124)

Groups

As I said earlier, you'll ideally find there are three groups. Which group you end up in initially is almost certainly down to how honest you've been with the organiser. If you tell them that you're a novice trackday rider then you'll hopefully end up in the novice group. If you find yourself sharing the track with a bunch of wild eyed MotoGP refugees then either they didn't listen or you weren't as clear, or honest, as you might have been. Or you've made a terrible mistake in your choice of organiser. Starting in the novice group is a Good Thing for lots of reasons. More than anything else, it means that you have no pressure on you whatsoever, and if you turn out to be quicker than the rest of the group then you can always move up. The rest of the riders in the group will be at a similar level of experience, and you'll all have a chance to learn from each other as well as to gain the maximum possible benefit. On the other hand, starting in the experienced group because you're a fast road rider could well result in your not enjoying the day as much, feeling under immense pressure and maybe even being asked to go to a slower group.

I mentioned an open pit lane earlier. Open pit lane means that there are no groups at all. Once you've passed scrutineering then you are free to go out onto the track whenever, and for however long, you wish. The only restriction is usually on the number of riders allowed out at a time. The cool thing about an open pit lane is that you're almost sure to get more track time in the day. The bad things are more numerous. You have no idea who you may be sharing the track with. You won't have the discipline enforced to make you come in and have a rest. And you may well spend ages at the pit lane exit waiting for someone to come in so that there's space for you on the track. Last time I went on an open pit lane track day I found myself sharing the circuit with a couple of British Superbike Championship contenders getting some extra practice time in on full blown race bikes as well as a 250cc GP rider. I'm experienced and fairly fast, and I was still way out of my depth...

Shared responsibilities

You're paying money to an organisation for them to arrange and run a professional trackday for you, so obviously they have certain responsibilities to you. But at the same time you have certain responsibilities to them and to your fellow riders.

It's only reasonable that you should expect the organisers to have the circuit booked, to lay on such marshalling and medical cover as is appropriate for the event and to organise proceedings during the day in a safe and controlled manner. But the organiser has the right to expect certain things from you. You need to be honest with them, both before you start and during the day. If you're nervous, if you feel that you're being pushed too hard or even if you have a complaint you need to tell the organiser so they can do something about it. Far better to swallow your pride and ask for help than to risk hurting yourself or someone else. The most important thing, though, is being honest at first and making sure you start off in the right group for you.

Green for go! You should see this on your first lap of a session and after you have passed a hazard (normally a yellow flag) to say you're free to play again!

Track rules and regulations

Compared to the road, these are few and far between. But they are there, and circumstances dictate that you stick to them for your safety and that of everyone else on the day.

Flags and marshals

When you're at the circuit you will see large numbers of people wearing bright orange jumpsuits. These are not in general escapees from a local institution but are, in fact, marshals. Marshals are among the most important and yet undervalued people in the motorsports arena. They are the first on the scene when something goes wrong and are the most likely reason why someone else's mishap doesn't become your catastrophe. Armed with flags, fire extinguishers and a rather dark sense of humour, marshals are also your direct contact with the people who run the circuit. They have a difficult and frequently thankless job and you'd be well advised to extend them some basic courtesy when you see them around. Marshals answer to the Clerk of the Course. The Clerk of the Course is The Boss. They have ultimate decision making ability – they can stop a session, exclude a rider, close the circuit for the day, pretty well anything. They are The Law on their circuit, and you would be wise not to incur their wrath.

On the track you'll see marshals at various points around the circuit, usually either in the doorway of small huts like sentry boxes or standing behind little extensions in the barrier. Their job is twofold - to manage situations when they occur, getting debris out of the way, slowing other riders down to avoid them getting involved and protecting the fallen rider and medical team from further harm; and to prevent situations from occurring by warning riders of hazardous track conditions or machine problems. They manage this with flags, and although you'll get a briefing at the beginning of your day explaining them it's probably worth going through the flags here as well.

Green Flag.
Something you should see on the first lap of your session and after you have passed a hazard such as a yellow flag to say all is well again.

I know the colours clash, but at least there's little chance of you honestly claiming not to see a marshal waving a yellow flag...

Yellow flag

Probably the most common event flag you'll see, the yellow means that there is a hazard ahead and you should approach with caution. That means slowing down and, in general anyway, not overtaking. It may be that someone has fallen off and they are on the circuit, it may be that someone has broken down, it may be anything. That's the point. The risk may not be on the track, it may be on the grass or gravel next to it – right where you'd end up if you got the corner wrong. So that's a hazard, for you and the recovery/medical team, and would get flagged. Riding past yellow flags at full speed is likely to result in your incurring someone's severe displeasure. It's also dangerous and inconsiderate, so it's best you don't do it.

Red flag.

Hopefully you'll never see it, but the red flag means that your session has been stopped early. The most common reason for this is someone falling off in a position where the only way the mess can be cleared up safely is if there is no traffic interfering or someone's engine has cried "enough" and dumped its contents all over the track. The two can, of course, be linked. If the red flags come out while you're on the track you should slow right down and be prepared to stop without much notice. When you reach the pitlane then leave the track. You also need to keep an eye out for emergency vehicles coming up behind you. Or parked across the track... If there's time then your session will usually restart after the incident is cleared up, so don't assume that a red flag means it's all over for the next 40 minutes.

Chequered flag.

The one you can guarantee seeing every session. The chequered flag means it's the end of your session. You've won. Yay for you. Finish your lap at a comfortable pace and pull into the pitlane when you get there. Standup wheelies across the line are generally discouraged and will probably result in a quiet chat with the organiser the first time and a slightly less quiet one with the Clerk of the Course if you do it again.

Tip

If you see the circuit ambulance waiting to come onto the track, DO NOT slam on your brakes and let it come on ahead of you. First of all, it's actually quicker for you to go past than it is for you to slow down. Second, when the ambulance reaches the incident you'll then have to filter past through less space, which is more dangerous. And finally, you have a very high probability of getting rear-ended by at least one rider behind you who isn't expecting you to be emergency stopping. Someone did that in front of me at an industry test day at Mallory Park. The ambulance driver was waving him past but all he could concentrate on was braking.

Unfortunately, I was about 2m behind him when he decided to stop. I was also on full throttle. It made things a little interesting for a few seconds...

Yes, he means you. Time to pop into the pits and see what the problem is.
Perhaps, if you're good, you can come out and play later...

Black flag.

This is one flag which, hopefully, you'll never see. The black flag, accompanied by a marshal pointing at you, means that there is a pressing reason why you should leave the circuit now. Slow down, get off the proper line and pull off when you get to the pitlane. There may be something wrong with your bike – it's very hard to see if you're leaking fluid from on board, for example, so for everyone's safety (including yours) you need to get it checked. It may be that there's something wrong with your kit – I've seen people black flagged because their helmet isn't done up, for example. Or it may be that the standard of your riding or behaviour is such that someone wishes to discuss it with you. In most cases, as soon as you get into the pit there will be someone to explain the problem. Once you've rectified it then you can get back out there and carry on with your session. Ignore a black flag and you'll find yourself giving the Clerk of the Course a jolly good listening to. You may also find yourself excluded from the rest of the day's riding or even banned from the circuit completely. Don't do it. Ever.

These days, the most common reason for a black flag is noise. Circuits have stringent noise limits placed on them by the local council. It's not something they decide on themselves. For some bizarre reason, in the UK a person can move into a house next door to a long established racetrack, complain about the noise and the council will slap restrictions on the circuit instead of doing the sensible thing and pointing out that the track was there before the person bought the house... You end up with stupid situations like Donington Park, where the low noise limits are enthusiastically enforced by the local authority in spite of the fact that the circuit is directly below the approach to East Midlands Airport with its regular stream of commercial airliners. All of which make considerably more noise than even the noisiest motorbike. But I digress. Check with the organisers to see if it's a noisy or quiet session you're booked on and make sure your bike complies. Getting chucked off (or worse still, not being allowed to start) because of a loud pipe is a frustrating and expensive waste of a day, and not recommended.

Personal equipment

You're riding on a racetrack and you will hopefully be going reasonably quickly at some point. So it should come as no surprise to learn that jeans aren't acceptable. A few circuits will allow you to wear Gore-Tex or similar, but most insist on leather. Not just a jacket and jeans, either – your leathers must have a zip securing the jacket to the trousers and you must have that zip done up whenever you're on the track. For information, by the way, two piece leathers are no longer acceptable for racing, even with full waist zips – it's one piece or nothing. While that isn't the case for trackdays, at least not yet, it's something to bear in mind. Race regulations, after all, are far more grounded in common sense than those imposed on road riders. It should also be fairly obvious what else you'll need. Gloves, boots and a full face helmet are all mandatory. Your helmet must be BSI or CE approved, and should ideally have an ACU sticker as well. It needs to be in reasonable condition, free of obvious chips and damage and with a secure fastening mechanism. Your visor also needs to be in reasonable condition, not totally opaque with scratches.

That's the bare minimum you need. You'd be seriously recommended to consider, or even better to actually use, a back protector and to invest in some proper race gloves and boots. A back protector because although there's no roadside furniture to hit if it does all go wrong, there are other bikes and the ground to worry about. Oh, and those little, gently curved kerbstones really hurt when you bounce across them at some ungodly speed on the way into the gravel trap. Race gloves and boots are both recommended because hands and feet are easy to break and hard to fix, so anything you can do to minimise your risk has to be a Good Idea. Plus they are designed for the type of riding you are eventually going to do and so will be more comfortable than most alternatives.

Your bike

Oddly enough, this is quite important. Now who'd have guessed? But what isn't important is the type of bike. I've seen people do trackdays on all sorts of bizarre machinery, and I've done a few on bikes you wouldn't expect myself. You can have a laugh on anything as long as you recognise its limitations. But the important thing is that it isn't mandatory to have a sports bike just because it's a track day. You shouldn't be too astonished when you get there to see that the majority of bikes will be distinctly sporty, but there will almost certainly be a couple of naked bikes, one or two classics and at least one oddity there. The only bike I've ever baulked at riding fast on a track was a fully dressed tourer which felt distinctly unstable and had almost no ground clearance at all. It was fast enough, but cornering was an exercise in metalwork as well as direction changing, and it really wasn't much fun. But all you actually need is bike which will pass scrutineering (more on that later) and with which you're happy and confident. It needn't necessarily be road legal, either, though of course you have to get it to the circuit and back. You should, out of basic courtesy, check with the trackday organiser before bringing a race bike to one of their sessions, as some don't really like it. But there's no real reason why you couldn't turn up on a full blown MotoGP bike as long as you make sure it isn't too noisy.

As an aside, I once turned up on a trackday at Brands Hatch on a BMW 1100 GS, complete with semi-knobbly tyres. While the handling was a little vague, it was good enough for me to lap a bloke on a Fireblade, passing him for the second time in the session around the outside at Clearways when he had his knee down and I was riding like a copper. Laugh? I should say so. Though he didn't see the funny side at all...

*It's big and it's clever. A trackday on an inappropriate
motorbike can be an enormous amount of fun...*

There are a few things that it's useful to remember when it comes to your choice of bike. A lot of people, myself included, get their biggest track kicks out of corner speed and huge lean angles. The reasoning is that any fool can go fast in a straight line. Hell, you can even do that in a car. But really committed cornering is an art, and there's almost nothing more satisfying. Now with that in mind there is a school of thought that naturally favours agile, lightweight bikes with brilliant cornering abilities but perhaps a slight lack of pace on long straights. 250cc two strokes and imported 400s tend to rule with this group. There's a group with another approach – that a trackday is all about going fast. This group generally favours litre class sportsbikes and will most commonly be seen hurtling down straights before scrubbing off rather more speed than absolutely necessary for the next corner. These first two groups tend to antagonise each other as the slower cornering 'fast' bikes get in the way of the faster cornering 'slow' ones, robbing them of corner speed, while the slower bikes will often pass the faster ones mid corner (or under braking) and stop them from getting the drive out of the corner to get that high speed rush. There is, of course, a third group. It's somewhat smaller and consists of people on

Nondescript bike, no flashy leathers, perfect positioning and going like the clappers. That'll be a member of the third group, then...

very fast (but sometimes quite unlikely) bikes who hurtle down the straights before braking hard and scrubbing off just enough speed to get around the corner, getting on the power early and hurtling off again. They frequently don't look particularly fast until you try to keep up with them...

Insurance and licences

Insurance is simple. You don't need any. You can buy trackday insurance but it covers your bike only, and usually only deals with total losses. It's rather important to remember that your insurance does not have anything for third parties. And nor, of course, does anyone else's. This is an important point, and goes some way toward explaining why trackday etiquette is important enough to almost get a full chapter to itself. If you do end up in an incident involving another rider, either as the instigator or as an innocent bystander, then it can get complicated. But in a nutshell, your costs are down to you, and the other rider looks after his own costs. If you are able, agree something between you that maybe reflects more accurately on actual events then congratulations. Should you be the litigious type you should probably understand that you are unlikely to be successful in suing to recover your costs unless the other rider was clearly and indisputably worse than merely negligent.

Licensing, however, is a different matter. Just about any UK trackday you attend will need a full EU bike licence. And you'll need to produce it when you sign in. If you forget it you can normally get confirmation of your having a licence over the phone from DVLA but it will cost you and it's a level of stress you could probably do without first thing in the morning. Some circuits will accept an ACU licence instead, though some organisers will not. And some organisers will accept you if you've been disqualified, as long as you can still produce the tattered and smoking remains of your licence. But there's a simple rule of thumb. You need a full EU motorcycle licence which you can produce when you sign on at the circuit. If you don't have one or won't be able to produce it then you need to talk to the organiser as soon as you can – certainly before you go. If they're worth going with then they will either be able to tell you how to get around the problem or will tell you straight that it's not going to happen. Never go with a company who says they can bend the rules for you. You may well be a deserving case, but what about the others? Who knows what you may find yourself sharing the track with?

Scrutineering

One of the worst things that can happen on a trackday, or indeed in a race, is having someone's engine letting go and dumping oil everywhere. Mechanical derangements of any kind are bad news, ranging as they do from an inconvenience for the rider through to a major catastrophe as half the field crash out on the resulting oil slick. So it figures that avoiding a mechanical disaster is a smart move. Obviously the first stage is down to you and your maintenance (yes, we'll look at that later) but when you get to the circuit you'll need to convince the scrutineers that you, your bike and your kit are up to the challenge ahead of you. In racing, the scrutineers are responsible for making sure that machinery is safe and that it complies to the technical regulations appertaining to the particular race. They also deal with personal equipment, checking condition and fitness for purpose. Failing scrutineering is the ultimate ignominy for a racer, generally resulting as it does in instant exclusion from the race and massive piss-taking from the rest of the field. Who will probably know about it before you've even got back to your garage/tent/van.

Obviously things are slightly different for a trackday, but the principle is the same. If the scrutineers aren't happy then you don't get to play. Their word is final and they are notoriously incorruptible. There are certain key things that they'll be looking for, and you'll see soon enough that these key things appear throughout this book. That's because they're really important. Sufficiently so, in fact, that I'm going to break one of my conventions and do a list.

- *Tyres*
- *Brakes*
- *Head bearings*
- *Fork seals*
- *Handlebar movement*
- *Chain tension*

- *Rear suspension movement*
- *Engine/gearbox health*
- *Exhaust noise*
- *General condition*
- *Rider's equipment*
- *Rider's condition*

Rider's condition? Yes – the bike could be perfect, your kit could be great, but if you're massively hung over, doped up to the eyeballs with anti-histamines for your hay-fever or otherwise not really fit then you're a menace to yourself and everyone else on the track and you'll not be allowed out until you can convince the scrutineers that you've got yourself together.

In the paddock at Brands

On the day

OK, we've looked at the theory, you've found the right company, booked a trackday, prepared your bike and yourself and have now rolled up at the circuit, bright eyed, bushy tailed and ready to go. And, apart from those annoying butterflies, it feels great. What happens next?

First things first

The first thing you'll normally encounter when you ride in (or, if you're that way inclined, when you arrive with your bike on a trailer or in a van) is one of the organisers directing you to a scrutineering bay. Having read the section on scrutineering, this will hold no terrors for you and you'll be relaxed and happy as the scrutineer pronounces your bike healthy, affixes a sticker saying he's happy and points you in the direction of the paddock. As he's checking your bike over he'll remind you that you need fuel. Don't worry – everyone forgets it at least once. There'll be a petrol station reasonably close, and plenty of people will be able to direct you to it. Be aware that some circuits are a little off the beaten track and their local filling stations may not accept credit cards. So make sure you have cash or a cheque book (remember those?) with you. No, I'm not kidding. On circuit petrol is normally sold at captive audience prices, so while it's better than pushing the bike, if you can buy elsewhere you probably should.

Once you've been through scrutineering you'll go on to the paddock to park your bike. There may well be different areas for the different groups – it's worth checking with the scrutineer – so make sure you park in the right place. It's not just to be awkward. The paddock area is often fairly crowded and people get their timings mixed up. If everyone from a group is parked together then it's easy to tell if you're supposed to be on the track. If you come back from the loo and your bike's on its own then yep, you should be out there...

The first thing you'll need to do after parking up is to get yourself signed in. Someone should be able to point you in the right direction, but if in doubt head for the cafe – there'll always be someone in there who can help you, whether staff or another rider like you. Signing on is the time you show your driving licence, sign the waiver ("If I fall off I won't sue the track, the organiser or anyone else") and probably pay the balance of your fee. You may be given a wristband afterwards. Put it on. You may well need to show it every time you go on track, certainly you will for the first sessions.

The safety briefing

After you've signed in you'll need to attend the safety briefing. Regardless of how many trackdays you've done or how good you are, the safety briefing is mandatory. Some trackday companies don't issue the wristband until after the briefing as an added incentive to attend.

The safety briefing runs through a variety of things concerned, hardly surprisingly, with safety. While your primary objective may well be to have a great day, the safety of participants, track workers and instructors is the main goal of the organisers. And rightly so. So you'll get a reminder of what the flags are and what they mean. More importantly, you'll get told if there are any local quirks associated with them, like where to leave the circuit in the event of a red flag or where the noise tests are taken, for example. You'll also get introduced to your instructors, get a rundown on the general behaviour expected of you (more on that later) and any other late breaking information. You should also get some advice about timings, where to park in the paddock and so on.

Some track day companies put cones out beside the track as guides for braking points, turning points and apexes. If yours does they will probably give some recommendations about the cones. The main one is likely to be along the lines of "If you're not happy about braking or turning there then use your own judgement." It's good advice, and again we'll talk about cones, as well as braking and turning points, later on.

Food and drink

Something else that may well come up at the safety briefing is catering arrangements for the day. But advice on what you should or shouldn't consume is likely to be limited. Now I'm not a dietary expert and this isn't a healthy lifestyles guide. But there are some good ideas that it's probably worth passing on. Circuit catering is actually quite good, especially where there are proper cafes there. Mallory and Cadwell come immediately to mind as places where I would actually choose to eat. But all of them will offer proper food, especially the staples of biker/trucker cafes everywhere. And that's a double edged sword, because what may well be nice to eat and comfortably filling will get its own back later. And I'm not talking about your waistline, either.

A big meal, while being ever so tempting, needs digesting. Well, obviously. But digestion uses energy, which is why you get sleepy after a big lunch. Add that to a morning running on adrenaline, which is pretty tiring anyway, and a big lunch will have you dozing your way into the gravel traps in no time. Still, at least you'll be relaxed when you get there. No, your best bet is plenty of complex carbohydrate, which gives a nice steady energy release, in a fairly light meal. That translates to, for example, a baked potato with filling, pasta or something like that.

While we're at it, you might want to consider not consuming huge quantities of coffee or other caffeinated drinks. Because, while caffeine is a great stimulant and does help to wake you up, at some point you'll fall off that caffeine high and then you're just as tired as before, plus a bit. Also, of course, with the amount of adrenaline that will be coursing through you after each session, adding another stimulant just might make you behave like a toddler full of tartrazine. Scary. Water is the best thing, and lots of it. Even on a fairly cool day you'll get pretty warm muscling your bike around and concentrating that hard. Water is great for rehydrating without any side effects.

On the track

At last the time has come and it's your turn to get out there. A few last checks – helmet secure, leathers done up properly, wristband accessible to show the marshal, that sort of thing – and then it's time to go to the end of the pitlane while you wait to get cleared onto the track. You'll want to go to the toilet a few minutes before this, by the way. Parking up for a nervous wee while your group is assembling is considered bad form.

Sighting laps

Your first session of the day is likely to be shorter than the rest. Probably just 10 minutes instead of the normal 20. Lots of companies also operate a no overtaking policy for the first session. The idea is to give you a chance to see where the track goes, make note of any apex and braking markers that may have been put out there and to just shed some of the natural

Happily you won't be seeing any of these on the track. But that's no reason to go silly at this early stage of the day...

trepidation you may be feeling. There will almost certainly be instructors on the circuit at the same time, and they will be riding a pretty good line so following them will give you an idea of what will happen as you get quicker. They may well also literally point to where you should be on the track. The whole idea of this first session is to help you with your confidence while removing any pressure you may be feeling. There's no need to go fast, no overtaking, just a nice relaxing ten minutes ride. As you go around you'll start to get a feel for where everything goes, which is useful in helping you to relax and enjoy yourself. It'll also give you a chance to get used to the lack of visual cues that you're accustomed to seeing. You know, roadsigns, other vehicles, white lines on the road and so on. Some circuits are a little featureless and it can be quite disconcerting to realise that you have no idea what's coming next *and there's nothing to give you a clue.* Best get that out of the way at a leisurely pace, then.

The next stage

You've done your sighting session and have had an excited natter in the paddock with a bunch of other, equally hyper riders. If you smoke you've almost certainly had one. And if you're honest with yourself you've probably started to size up the others in your group to see who's slower than you and who you want to beat. That's OK – wanting to improve yourself is healthy. And the next two groups have gone out and done their thing, so it's nearly your turn again.

When you go out this time you'll notice an immediate difference. There is a certain frisson in the air. Many of your group will be riding quicker, and everyone seems to be more purposeful. Adrenaline is at a higher level than before. Because although the circuit is the same as before and the basic principle of what you're doing has remained the same, this time the rules have changed a little. Sure, there will generally still be instructors on the circuit, but that's about it. You can now ride at your own pace. Overtaking is on, and so, whether you like it or not, is the pressure. Because you've made that assessment – who's slower than you, who you want to beat – and now you're out to prove yourself right. And that's where it all starts to go wrong.

It's distressingly common for people to throw their bikes into the scenery on the first full session. Why? Because they get in over their heads, either through overconfidence or an overdose of (usually) testosterone. So, with that sobering thought, let's have a look at things you can do to avoid that early gravel bath.

Etiquette

Etiquette (*ettiket n*): the formal rules for polite behaviour in society or in a particular group.

That's actually not as inappropriate a term as you may imagine. Because although the trackday atmosphere is anything but formal, there are some fairly distinct rules which you need to observe if you wish to avoid some rather robust discussions at the end of the session. Or worse still, in the gravel trap.

Overtaking

Overtaking isn't frowned upon, generally, but there are some basic points of courtesy to remember. You aren't actually racing, so there are no championship points or prizes on offer for the winner. The overtaking rider is responsible for making sure that the overtake is safe. That means, in practice, overtaking where you're not going to interfere with the other rider doing something he needs to. Like getting into position for a corner. Or even taking the corner at all. So stuffing it down the inside before braking hard and slamming your bike in front of the other rider in a perfect block pass isn't on. Nor is driving out hard from a corner and running wide, pushing the other bloke onto the grass or forcing him to back off. In short, if you're going to pass someone then do it cleanly, safely and in the same way that you'd expect them to do it to you. Several companies will actually go so far as to prohibit riders from overtaking in the braking and turning zones, limiting passes to the far safer exits and straights. Even if yours doesn't, it's not a bad idea to restrict yourself to the same rules until you get a little more track time under your belt.

Of course, this not being a race, it doesn't matter if you get overtaken yourself. So it's also not done to make it harder than necessary for someone to pass you. Blocking, weaving and generally erratic riding is dangerous and could well see you on the receiving end of some distinctly unfriendly karma. Wobbling round a corner on your megabike, holding up someone who was polite enough to wait for a safe overtake and then pinning the throttle and flying down the straight, just to do it to them again at the next corner is perfectly acceptable though it might be considered discourteous to do it for more than a couple of laps. I once found myself in a session with a not very fast guy on a very fast bike. Each corner saw me having to roll off to avoid ramming him as he tottered around, but his bike was so quick that the straights allowed him to stay in front despite my best efforts. I knew he knew I was there and I knew he knew he was holding me up. Eventually I had to be rude and pass him mid corner, dropping down the inside and then getting the drive to stay in front (and, if I'm honest, blocking

Obviously this is racing so the rules are a little different, but this is a great example of how NOT to do a clean overtake. Laconi (55) has tried to pass Fabrizio (84) on the outside at the approach to Druid's at Brands Hatch. He's not left himself anywhere to go but hasn't got past either. So he turns in on Fabrizio.

At this point the bikes are touching. Fabrizio's front wheel is millimetres from getting jammed in Laconi's fairing and spitting them both off.

Somehow they both got away with it. This sort of behaviour would get you a serious talking at from the Clerk of the Course as well as generating some very hostile vibes from the rest of your group. Don't do it. Or be ready to apologise a lot if you do it by mistake.

him a bit) on the way out. Bad manners, yes, and potentially dangerous but made necessary by his selfish riding.

That last example brings me onto the next thing. Sometimes something will happen which results in a slightly robust overtake or someone having to brake harder than they'd like or whatever. If you feel you may have caused that sort of thing, go find the other rider and make sure there are no bad feelings to sour the next session. Or, worse still, to make someone do something daft. And if you were on the receiving end then go have a chat about it – chances are the other rider didn't realise anything was wrong and will be suitably apologetic. I got run off the track at Cadwell once when someone was banking on me to back off before entering a corner, thinking he was the only person in the session who didn't. Unfortunately, I didn't either so his line put him right in my way. No problem – I took an escape road and rejoined later. He came to find me after the session and we talked about it. No harm done, and we're now good friends.

Getting sucked into a race
While it's not really a breach of etiquette as such, it often leads to one. Or several. You've been in your group for a few sessions and you've started to get the pecking order sussed out. There are a couple of people around the same pace – though obviously not the same ability - as you and you find yourself catching one of them midway through a session. You know you're quicker so you decide it's time to pass and make your mark. The trouble is, he thinks the same way and doesn't want to yield. Now at this point one or other of you is at, or very close to, their personal limit. The other isn't as close. We all need to find our limits, of course, as that's the only way we expand them, but this may not be the best way to do it. Because if you really are the faster then you're going to get past. Probably. But your rival is going to be pushing beyond his own limits and getting ragged. That'll make it easier for you to pass, perhaps. Especially as he screws up his braking for a corner and runs wide. Hell, even the best do that occasionally. But the more likely scenario is that you'll both push harder and harder, and will both find yourselves going beyond your limits. Then beyond the little stretch outside your comfort zone that is beneficial to learning and into the grey area where you're just surviving. It's stopped being fun, you're no longer concerned about anything other than getting past, or staying ahead of, that other bike. Overtakes are made with reckless abandon, braking gets harder and later and you're on the gas earlier and earlier. Perhaps you'll be lucky and you'll both get to the end of the session, to be rewarded with a huge hit of Dopamine as your body rewards you for surviving. You'll have a great laugh with your protagonist and you will, in fact, have learned a little. But it's also quite possible, likely even, that one

or other of you will overcook it and go gravel surfing. The most likely thing will be to try to outbrake the other guy and either lose the front or simply run out of track, but there's also a good chance of sliding out as you try to carry too much speed through the corner or highsiding as you get on the power on the way out. None of them are a pleasant experience.

But the biggest single breach in etiquette you can make on a trackday is to involve another rider in your accident. Mistakes happen, of course, and the fact that there are a number of you riding in a group increases the risk of an off becoming a community event. But in spite of that, it's rare indeed that someone will get taken out by another rider. The main reason can be found just a paragraph or two back. The most common places for people to come off are on the approach/turn in and mid corner. And these are the places where you are encouraged not to be overtaking. That lifts the pressure to brake deeper and harder as well as giving that essential bit of space to allow you to have your accident in peace. Of course, when the red mist is down and you're deep into your private GP, that's the last thing on your mind. Fortunately it's still difficult to take someone out, though crashing in front of them will certainly sharpen their concentration rather...

Falling off

Generally considered rather bad manners as it means that the rest of your group have to, at best, slow right down on what must be an interesting part of the track (otherwise you wouldn't have come off there, right?) and at worst have their session stopped. So if you can avoid it you should try to do so.

Wheelies, stoppies and burnouts

It's probably worth pointing out that although they don't really count as breaches of etiquette as such, wheelies and stoppies are certainly not approved of by circuit officials and are likely to earn you a chat if you're seen doing them. The exceptions that come to mind are Donington Park

Coming over The Mountain at Cadwell Park is one place where wheelies are almost unavoidable. Even when you're being restrained like this guy...

and the full circuits at Mallory Park and Brands Hatch, where there are points at which it is hard not to lift the front if you are travelling at a reasonable pace.

Burnouts will probably land you with a bill for any damage to the tarmac as well as risk you getting sent off for having a bald or inappropriately worn rear tyre.

Ignoring marshalls

There is, of course, one other major *faux pas* you can commit. Marshals waving flags are not generally doing so for the exercise or as training for a cheerleader competition. No, they are doing it to attract your attention. In your safety briefing, and in the explanation earlier in this book, you will have noticed a common phrase linking almost every single one of the flags. That phrase was slow down. Going past a flag-waving marshal head down, throttle pinned is possibly the ultimate sin in that you are genuinely putting people's lives at risk through your own inattention. You will almost certainly get a thorough talking at by the organisers or the Clerk of the Course, and if you're a repeat offender or are not sufficiently contrite then you may well find yourself summarily thrown off the track. It is, quite simply, inexcusable.

The end of the session

All good things must come to an end, and your trackday session in no exception. The chances are you will have no idea how long you've been on the track, and the appearance of the chequered flag will come as a complete surprise. The first thing to remember is that, depending on the circuit, you still have almost a complete lap of your session left. There is no requirement to slow down until you approach the entrance to the pitlane, though you may choose to use these last few moments as an opportunity to let everything cool down a bit before stopping. Whether you decide to cruise it or take it at full speed, though, you should keep in mind that not everyone in the group will necessarily have made the same decision. So be aware that you may either be coming up on people going far slower than you or that you may have much faster riders coming up behind you. Personally, I treat the first part of the final lap as any other and then back off for the last couple of corners before the pitlane.

It's a good idea, though not compulsory, to adopt the racer's technique of putting your left arm up in the air when you've slowed down. It's a clear signal to anyone behind you that you're not running at full pace and avoids

Slowing down for the pitlane entry, this rider has his hand up to warn anyone behind him. He's an instructor (hence the dayglo vest) so we should expect good behaviour from him, right?

confusion. Or getting rammed up the backside by someone who isn't quite as on the ball as you are.

There will probably be a marshal at the pitlane entrance with a red flag, waving you in. You are extremely unlikely to miss the entrance, but if you do then take the next lap very slowly and expect to get a stiff talking to later on. Yes, it's wise to keep concentrating even at this stage.

Oh, and as I said in the rules bit, victory celebrations on taking the chequered flag are generally frowned upon. Just give yourself a cheer inside your helmet and store it up for later.

Riding on the track

It goes without saying that the vast majority of what you have learned so far about riding a motorbike on the road applies equally well on the track. The throttle still works the same way, as do the brakes. You still use the same technique to get the bike turned and to keep it there. So what's so different? In truth, nothing needs to be different at all, and if you've come on a trackday simply to hone your machine control skills then you can make enormous gains without really changing anything, simply by pushing the envelope a little. But at the same time you can develop your skills and take a more track oriented approach which can also translate to your daily riding in the real world.

The caveat

Before you go any further, though, please read this paragraph and make sure you understand it. During this chapter, and later on, I will suggest some exercises you can try, either to demonstrate how things happen or to help you to tackle different elements of track riding. It seems a reasonable assumption that you are of sufficient age and intelligence to ride a motorcycle legally and to have responsibility for your actions. So please, make sure, when and if you try any of the exercises suggested, that it is safe to do so. If you are uncomfortable with anything suggested then simply don't do it. The choice, and responsibility, is entirely yours.

You

The biggest influence on how fast, how smoothly and how safely you can ride, whether on the track or on the road, is you yourself. You decide when to brake, when to turn, when to open the throttle, but your approach to all these things decides how effective they are. Not just your mental approach, which we've already touched on, but your physical one.

The most important part of your bike, for performance, safety, everything, is you, the rider. We've already touched on this when we've looked at attitude and so on, and there's no need to go back over all that. But there's more than attitude at stake here – though the key is how you've got your head working, how you sit and move on the bike makes a huge difference to how everything comes together on the track.

Let's get one thing straight. If you don't want to climb around and hang off, there's absolutely no requirement for you to do so. None at all. The bike will go around a corner without you moving off the seat one iota. But if you're going to get the most out of what your bike is capable of then there are a few key things you can do to help.

Relax

You are a significant proportion of the total weight of your bike. I'm not being rude – an average sized bloke weighs roughly half a modern sportsbike. So even if you're a small person on some sort of leviathan you're probably going to be the best part of a third of the weight of your bike – a quarter of the total package. Bear that in mind while we look at relaxing. Everything will become clear shortly. Take braking as an example. You hit the brakes and go rigid. Your arms are now transmitting maybe 20% extra weight to the forks and thence to the front tyre. That's 20% more dead weight pushing your front tyre into breaking away. Locking your arms directly reduces your front suspension's ability to deal with what's being thrown at it – compression under braking, bumps, everything. And that's a Bad Thing.

But it's not the only thing. Let's assume that you've made it to the corner and started to turn. Your stiff, rigid arms are now stopping the bike from turning, and although you're not actually strong enough to prevent the turn from happening, provided you've done the basic essentials of course, you're making it about as difficult as possible. Oh, and that stiff, rigid body is now putting a big chunk of weight high above your bike's centre of gravity, reducing stability and making those rigid arms even more disastrous.

It gets better. Your muscles are bunched and tense, and you're working much harder than you need to. After a lap or two you've probably started to get sore shoulders and a tension headache is just around the corner. So to speak. In short, you're almost certainly not having a very good time. And that's a bit of a waste of your time and money.

So let's get you relaxed. You can start off by doing some exercises if you want. Find out what it feels like to be tense. Sit on your bike, engine off, and work your way through your body, tensing each group of muscles and then relaxing them again. It feels, and looks, slightly daft, but it's a great way of forcing yourself both to relax and to recognise the signs of getting tense. Oh, and if you can keep a smile while you're doing it and overcome the self conscious feeling that inevitably accompanies this exercise then you're well on the way to being relaxed.

Looking down a few metres in front of the bike, arms locked and running wide... Not a happy chappy – and it shows

Once you're on the bike and moving, try to smile. Really. You're supposed to be enjoying yourself, after all. But if you're smiling then it's harder to tense up. If you're still tense then pop your tongue between your teeth. One of two things happens. You relax or you bite your tongue. It's really quite an easy choice to make. Once you're out there, if you find you really, truly can't relax then there's one last thing to do. Slow down, run at a pace where you're comfortable for a bit and then allow things to pick up in their own time.

If you're on something vaguely sporty, or if you want to adopt a sporty riding position as you increase speed, it's really useful to try to keep your forearms parallel to the ground. You'll never really manage it, but having the intention, and the general direction, makes a massive difference to both your riding position and to the likelihood of your arms staying bent and you staying relaxed.

Look where you're going

It sounds obvious, doesn't it? But it's something that people simply don't do properly. It's easy to confuse looking where you're pointed with looking where you're going. Especially when the pace is starting to hot up. It's also a great way to tell when someone is going too far outside their comfort zone. Stand by the track and watch – you'll see some riders who are looking at the track a couple of metres in front of their bike. They've generally got stiff arms and are emitting an aura of utter discomfort – you don't need to be some sort of psychic to see it either, just read the body language and it becomes pretty clear, to be honest.

So although it's part of the relaxation thing, there's more to it than that. When you're riding on the road you're looking a fair way ahead, assessing risk and assimilating lots of information. Hopefully. If you're not then you need help before you become a statistic. But that's a different matter. On the track you're probably fine at moderate speed. There's not so much to take in for a start – nothing coming the other way, no road signs, no turnings to take or directions to think about – and you're having no problem in taking on all that's going on around you. But as speed picks up and you approach the edge of your comfort zone you start to narrow your field of view. Tunnel vision. You also start to bring your attention point closer to you. You're too busy to process all that additional information so you just narrow your focus more and more. Eventually you're looking at a spot just in front of your bike. Of course, you're not spotting things until it's too late to do anything about them, so your riding gets more ragged, you get more overloaded and the whole thing feeds itself. *(see over for illustrations)*

So you're coming up to a corner. Keep your head up and look deep into the corner. As soon as you've identified your turn in point then look at the apex. If you can't see it then look towards it. As soon as you've got yourself pointed at the apex look for the exit, and as soon as you've found the exit look on down the track. This sounds harder than it is. But it does make life easier for you: it gives you time to see what's coming up and to get ready to deal with it. It also puts your body in the right position for whatever your bike is doing.

We're at the turn-in for Graham Hill at Brands Hatch. Above you can see where the bike should be pointed, while below shows where you should be looking. Kind of gives you more time to plan things, doesn't it?

Same thing, this time at the apex. Direction of travel above, direction of eyes below. Look at the buildings to see how much further you can see. Oh, the view is slightly funny because of course if you're really getting the apex then your eyes are over the grass inside the corner.

A different corner, but it makes the point. That yellow cone is the apex marker. Look where the rider is looking, even at this early stage...

Turned in and heading for that late apex. Which she's still looking at...

Still turning, still focussed...

And just out of shot is that cone. She's looking at the exit now...

Move your body

No, this isn't about getting your knee down or anything like it. We can look at that later. No, in this section we're simply looking at using that weight we spoke about earlier to your advantage. You're approaching that bend again and looking deep into the corner, just as explained before. You've turned your head, of course, and because you're keeping your head up to maximise the distance you're looking into the corner, your upper body has started to twist. That means that you're moving your weight towards the inside of the corner, and this is a Good Thing. If you've managed to keep your arms bent as well then you're doing even better. Your weight is over the front end of the bike but with bent arms you're not interfering with the suspension or steering, just helping with weight distribution. You can help to make sure your arms stay bent by consciously dropping your inside shoulder into the corner as well. It will encourage bent elbows as well as getting your weight further towards the inside of the turn – exactly where you want it to be.

Leaning the wrong way - the bike is leant over but the weight is high. Looks unnatural, doesn't it. And it feels pretty odd, too.

The first time I went to the Nurburgring was on a course. My instructor was a retired policeman on a fairly tatty looking Honda Fireblade and I was on a ZX6-R Kawasaki. It's a real eye opener to follow someone round a fast corner, knee, toe and calf sliders all grinding away happily when the guy you're following hasn't even stuck his knee out. And he hasn't actually got sliders on his leathers. But he'd move his upper body a fair amount, and his positioning, lines and bike control were impeccable. So you can corner just as fast with a good technique as you can by impersonating a gibbon. Though it doesn't look as cool...

Your body, of course, is a whole lot more than just your arms and shoulders. Your lower body has a part to play as well. Especially your legs. Because if you're nice and relaxed and you've got your elbows bent and everything else is the same as usual, the first time you brake hard two things will happen. Two things, that is, that you weren't expecting. First of all you will headbutt the clocks and/or screen as you flop forwards. And secondly you will ram your groin into the back of the tank as you slide forwards on the seat. Neither of these are generally considered to be either good form or beneficial to cornering. So you need to grip the tank with your knees – it's usually contoured to make that easier for you – which will stop you from ending up on top of it, and you need to use your stomach muscles to keep your face off the speedo. No, you don't need to develop a six pack, you just need to plan ahead and be ready for your braking when it comes. You can practice easily by simply riding along as normal and taking one hand off the bars without sitting up or wobbling. You'll find that you are taking a proportion of your weight with your stomach muscles. If it's safe and you're feeling adventurous then try going a little quicker (to stay stable) and then taking both hands off the bars, holding your position with your stomach. Don't just sit up as that doesn't achieve anything. The idea is for you to see that you can easily support your weight in your normal riding position without using your arms.

As an aside, on the road and on the track the more of your weight you can keep off the bars then the better your bike will steer and the more comfortable the ride will be as the suspension is freer to work. Plus you get a free abs workout.

While we're talking about moving, by the way, you can make life easier for yourself in lots of ways by moving around. For example, you're hurtling down a straight, tucked in behind the screen and being aerodynamic. Now at some point you're going to have to brake. You can stay tucked in, of course, but that's a little pointless when you can sit up and instantly get an air brake to help you lose speed. Also, by sitting up you can ease some weight backwards so the rear stays down longer and you can brake harder.

Then, when you're nailing it out of the corner, if you start to tuck in again then you're putting weight over the front wheel, keeping it down as you accelerate, as well as being in the most aerodynamic position for when you're going quickly enough for that to matter. You've also had to bend your arms, by the way. . .

Arms bent, knees gripping the tank and already looking deep into the corner. Perfection. Look at how the forks are compressed to give an idea of how hard he's braking – and at how confident he must be.

Using all the track

The biggest mistake that new track riders make is not using the whole track. And it really is a mistake, as by limiting yourself to, say, two thirds of the circuit width then you are limiting your cornering ability, as well as putting an unnecessary pressure on yourself. Your organiser has rented the entire circuit for the day, and it's rude not to use it all. So on a left hander get yourself right over to the right hand edge before turning in, take the apex right over on the left and allow yourself to run all the way back out on the exit. Doing it this way increases the radius of the turn,

In the braking zone for Graham Hill again. Notice that we're right over on the edge of the track.

At the apex. Over on the other side of the track, kissing the kerb. Not literally.

At the exit, all the way back across the track and hard on the power.

allowing you to carry more speed through the corner and to get on the power earlier. If the organiser has put out cones to mark entry points and apexes, they will have assumed that you are riding the whole track. The entry points won't work if you're in the middle of the track – you'll end up turning too early and threepenny-bitting (or twenty pence piecing if that's an easier image) as you pick it up, start to go wide, turn again, get too tight and so on. As you get quicker you'll find it less and less enjoyable, and you'll also find that you're running out of ground clearance and it's all getting a little more exciting than you need.

It may feel ridiculous using the whole track at first, but force yourself to ride the correct line, even when you're clearly not going fast enough to need to do so. Then you can get used to where you should be when the pace is comfortable and as you start to wind the wick up a bit it will be one less thing to concentrate on – and it will suddenly start to feel utterly natural to swoop through a bend from kerb to kerb.

Translating it to road use, using the whole road gives you the maximum visibility into the corner, allowing you the luxury of, perhaps,being able to tell if there's anything coming the other way and giving you the maximum safety margin. On the road you generally turn in later than on the track, as well as probably not going so fast, so your exit won't carry you so wide either. Obviously it's not always possible to use all the road, but you can certainly use all your lane most of the time and quite a lot more some of the time.

Something to be wary of, though, both on some circuits and on the road, is raised kerbs. Clipping the apex is all well and good, but hitting a raised kerb with your engine cases or, even worse, your knee is really not something you'll want to do more than once. Also bear in mind that the kerbs, whether raised or not, will be slippery as anything if they are wet. So stay off them if it's a rainy session.

Cornering

The daddy. The reason most of you will have even considered a trackday. Cornering is the single most important thing you can learn to do on a motorbike, and cornering well on the track is possibly the most satisfying thing you can do while still dressed. Whether you are a proponent of the Mike Hailwood 'keep it clean' style or whether you advocate hanging off like a baboon, the track is the place to refine your cornering technique to the point where you can deal with anything that the real world can throw at you. It's a sad reflection on our abilities as bikers that the majority of us who get it severely wrong out on the road do it all on our own, and we do it by failing to get around corners. Most commonly, most depressingly, we don't even try. Our brain says we're going too fast and we either brake or just give up, when almost every time we would in fact have got around with something still left in reserve. So trackdays, even if you have no interest in increasing your speed, are the perfect opportunity to find what your limits are, confirm that they are well within those of your bike (they almost certainly will be) and to get a better idea of what you can do when you miscalculate the severity or duration of a bend and you really have to exercise your new found skills!

A corner starts way before you've reached it. In fact, as soon as you know there's a corner coming up then you should be starting to take it. Because the two key things you need to get right, the elements without which your corner won't be the piece of art that it deserves to be, are *positioning* and *speed*. We've talked about using the whole track already, but it's worth re-iterating the point. If you're not using the whole track then you are compromising the whole corner, which means that you're neither going as quickly as you could be nor leaving the safety margin you ought to have.

So let's assume that the corner we're dealing with here is the simplest of all – a constant radius right hander approached from a nice long straight, and that you have the track to yourself. Now let's have a look at what ou're going to do.

The first step is to recognise that there is a corner coming up. It sounds obvious, but it's part of the plan, and a plan is a good thing. Next you're going to identify your braking point from the information you already have about the corner – whether you've already done it a hundred times or whether it's your first and you're reading the physical signs to get an idea of how tight it is, how long it goes on and so on. Or simply using the cones your trackday organiser has put out. While you're doing this you can start to adjust your position on the track so you're in the right place when you turn in. For a simple corner like this (see over the page), the right place is on the outside of the track – the left in this case. Your braking point at this stage will be quite a lot earlier than necessary. That's OK – we'll look at that later but for now it's far better that you arrive with speed in hand than with lots more braking still to do.

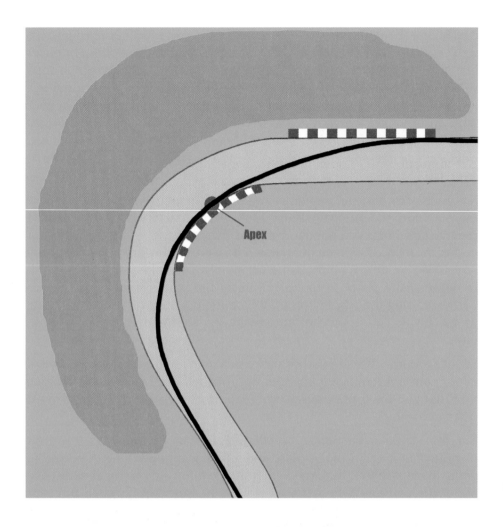

Apex

So, let's look at the digram above. You're over on the left and thundering down towards your corner. Make sure you really are over to the left. Not quite brushing the grass, but pretty close. I've lost count of the number of people I've seen whose idea of being across to the outside of the track is riding about a metre off the centreline... Your turn in point is rather later than you would naturally guess, and the apex of the corner, the dot, is a little more than halfway round. Why? Because you're going more slowly at the beginning of the corner than at the end, so instead of prescribing a perfect arc, your course through the turn is flattened, with the radius increasing at the end. Also, turning later and apexing later means the bike is stood up and going straight earlier so you can get on the power sooner. One day this will matter to you....In this simple corner you can see the apex from the turn in point, so peel in when you feel it's right (or at the cone if there is one) and aim for the apex. Try to make it one smooth sweep in. Once you reach the apex and you can see your exit, start putting the power on and allow the bike to run out to the outside of the track as you clear the corner.

Turning and countersteering

Cornering doesn't happen unless you get the bike turned. Obviously. And you almost certainly already know that you don't turn by leaning, although the bike won't turn without being leant over. To get your head around this bit you need to remember that your wheels are a pair of big gyroscopes and will always behave accordingly.

Still turning into the apex, relaxed and looking through the corner, the author attempts to practice what he preaches (Photographer unknown)

You're not heavy enough to make a huge difference to things on a reasonable sized bike when it's in a stable state like, say, going in a straight line. If you lean your body, even though the bike will do something, it will take an age to start turning. Yet you always manage to get leant over and turning quite quickly. You're using something called gyroscopic precession, and it's a law of physics which says that if you tilt a gyroscope it will exert a force at 90° to the direction you've tried to tilt it. So if you try to push the front of your front wheel left, for example, it will actually tilt the wheel to the right. Why? Because precession has tried to push the bottom of the wheel left (force at 90° in the direction of rotation) and friction with the ground has prevented it from moving that way. So the top of the wheel ends up going right instead. It doesn't take a rocket scientist to work out that if you're pushing the front of the wheel left, the back is being pushed right, so precession gives you more force leaning the bike over to one side than you'd expect. You can prove I'm not talking nonsense by riding along in a straight line at 30-40mph and, when it's safe, pushing the bars gently one way or another. You will, if you're doubting me, be surprised by the result. Yes, you'll turn in the opposite direction to the way you turned the bars. And you'll turn pretty sharply, too, so make sure that you're ready to catch it and that you've got the room to muck about.

Gyroscopic forces are fantastically strong, so you can use this technique to speed up the rate that you can get the bike leaned over and turning. You already do, of course, but may not realise it. Learn to countersteer consciously and your cornering will improve and become much more precise.

Braking and slow in, fast out

One of the biggest things people do wrong on trackdays, on the road, even in racing, is approaching a corner too fast. Too much speed on the way in will rob you of speed on the way out, it will also compromise your line and make you rush things. Worst case, it will force you to step outside the limits imposed by physics, at which point the potential for it all to get a little over-exciting becomes very high. We all want to corner faster, especially on the track, but the way to approach the limit for any particular corner/bike/rider combination is from below. Running through a bend and thinking you could have gone quicker is infinitely preferable to lying in the gravel thinking that perhaps that was a little too ambitious. So build up your speed during the course of a few sessions but remember to try to force yourself onto the proper line, even if you don't need it yet.

Braking is, in its simplest form, a very straightforward exercise. Grab the front lever and squeeze while stepping on the rear pedal. Of course, there's more to it than that. The key things are to be smooth, to keep your elbows bent and to brake as though you mean it. Your tyres will absorb an astonishing amount of punishment before yielding grip, though any half decent modern bike should still be able to overwhelm them, but to give them a sporting chance it's best to build braking force up over a short time rather than just grabbing a handful. Keeping your elbows bent allows them to absorb some of the force of you pushing down through the bars as well as helping the suspension to keep working, while sitting up helps your body to act as an air brake for some added assistance.

If you're really serious about braking then you need to go from no brakes to absolute maximum in well under a second. As soon as you start to brake your centre of gravity moves forward and you start to put more weight on the front tyre. More weight at this stage means that it's less likely to lock so you can put more braking effort in which puts more weight on the front which means you can brake harder and so on. Eventually you'll brake so hard that your back wheel will lift off the ground. This is your limit – brake any harder than that and you will have left the realms of trying to stop fast and have become a stunt rider. Or a human cannonball. It depends how good you are. It is possible that your front wheel will lock before you reach this point, though, especially if your bike has fairly lazy steering geometry or slightly dodgy tyres. Obviously this is also a limit. Get off the brakes straight away and you should be fine. Stay on them and you will almost certainly fall off.

If you're feeling brave and curious then you can deliberately lock your front wheel. It may be useful for you to see that the technique for recovering from this rather unpleasant situation does work, as well as feeling what a locked front is like and seeing what makes it happen. But I'm not entirely convinced, and am including the exercise as a theoretical one. To lock your front wheel, get up to about 30mph on a clear, straight piece of tarmac. If it isn't on the public highway that is probably a good thing in case it all goes wrong. Make sure you're going in a straight line, get settled and really grab the front brake, letting it off immediately. If it locked then well done. You may have felt the front start to tuck in and felt distinctly uncomfortable, or it may all have stayed lovely and stable. Either way, releasing immediately makes the exercise fairly safe as there isn't really time for it to get out of hand. If the wheel didn't lock then try again but grab harder and faster. The two reasons why the wheel may not lock are insufficient pressure and too slow application. The useful thing is that you get to see just how hard and fast you really can brake before locking up.

Eventually you'll get confident enough that you'll be able to leave little rubber dashes with your front tyre all the way down to standstill as you lock, release, lock, release and so on.

You can do the same with the rear if you want. Same as before, get up to speed, get steady and then just stamp on the back. It will almost certainly lock but should be far less dramatic. Indeed, if you want you should be able to ride the locked rear all the way to standstill. Bear in mind that you'll not do your tyres any good and that your ability to turn is highly compromised while the wheel is skidding.

So let's get back to the corner and look at a couple of alternative scenarios. Rider A brakes gently, scrubs off a little speed and turns in at the normal point. At this stage he's going maybe 20mph too fast for his perceived

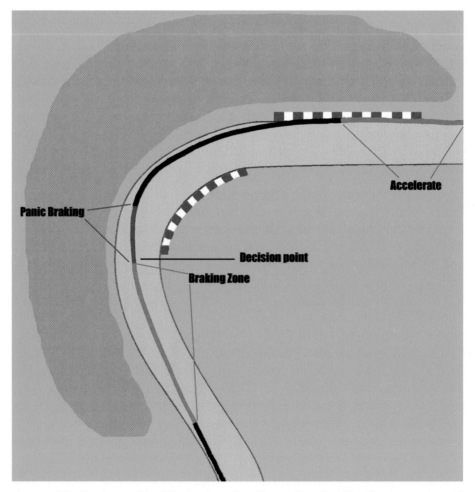

Approaching too fast and braking too late, the rider realises that it's all going wrong and hits the anchors. A brief moment of panic and he loses enough speed to get turned in, still on a closed throttle. Nasty.

cornering ability. Maybe he can still get round, but in his head he can't. So he needs to lose some speed but he's leaned over as far as he thinks he can go and yet he still has to slow down. He shuts the throttle first, of course, which unsettles the back, causing the rear to pitch and wallow a little and affecting his confidence further. Now at this stage he has three choices. Force himself to turn tighter, run off the edge of the track or brake while cranked right over. Of these three, only the first one has any potential long term benefit. The others offer varying degrees of discomfort and pain, but none of them are going to feel very nice at the time. Let's assume that he gets round the corner with the lightest application of the brakes, though.

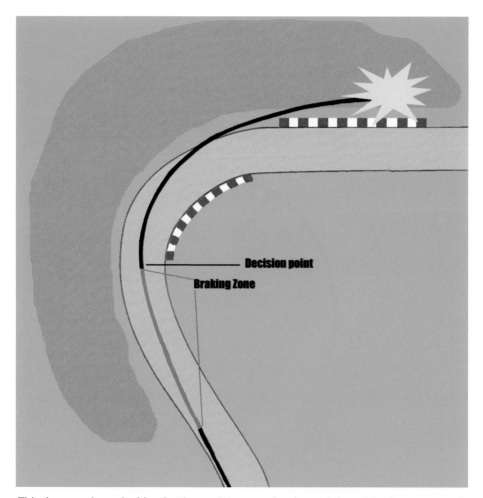

This time, our hero decides that he can't turn any harder and daren't brake any more. In this case he's probably going much, much too fast, and he's lucky to drop it at low speed a few feet into the gravel.

We like a happy ending, right? So now as the corner starts to open up he's got to go from a completely closed throttle to getting power on for the next straight. Again the bike gets unsettled and there's a good chance he'll be in the wrong gear as well, so progress down the straight won't be as good as it could be. Plus, of course, his heart is in his mouth and his confidence is in tatters.

Now let's look at rider B. He's braked more, turned in at the same point but is going maybe 10mph slower than he ought to be. As he turns in he will see very quickly that he's got space and speed to spare, so he can stay on a positive throttle, keeping the rear suspension slightly loaded, the back

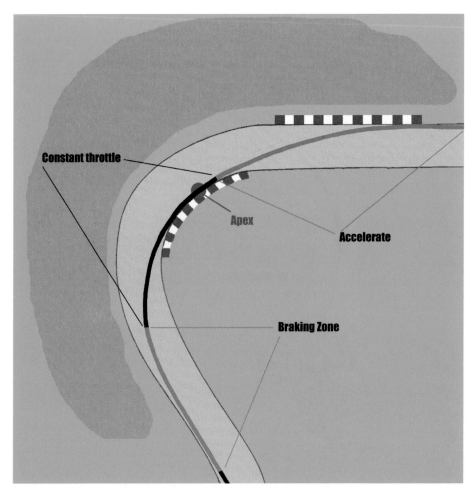

A more cautious approach leads to the minimum of time off the throttle and clean, progressive acceleration all the way out. It's faster, safer and better looking – how much more can you ask?

tyre digging in nicely and everything feeling taut and positive. He's not really accelerating as such, just maintaining drive. Then, as the corner opens up, he can smoothly feed the power in and get the perfect launch down the straight. In racing, the exit to the last corner before the main straight is the most important point on the circuit, as a mistake there can cost you maybe 20mph by halfway down, and that's a huge difference.

Rider A will also be slower on the next lap as he's scared himself. Maybe that slowing down will actually make him quicker as next time he'll be like rider B. Rider B on the other hand has decided he can go a little quicker and ramps it up by a few mph, sees that still works and carries on getting gradually faster but with a decent safety margin.

Self assessment

In your mind you're cranked right over, footpegs millimetres off the ground and absolutely at the bike's limit. Or perhaps you see yourself as barely leaning over at all, with acres of ground clearance to spare. In fact, on both occasions you're somewhere just over halfway in to the bike's capabilities. And, therefore, yours. If there was a single thing that I would blame for the majority of riders coming to grief, whether on the road or

This guy is going to have a problem if that bend gets any tighter – he doesn't think he can turn any more...

the track, it's the difference between their perception of how hard they are leaned over and how far they actually are leaning.

If you think that you're at the limit then you won't try to turn harder. Because you can't – you're at the limit. So you do something else. And if you're needing to turn tighter because you've overcooked a corner or you need to change your line but you can't lean any more then your options are a little limited. Braking when you're leaned over is the province of the brave, the skilled and the foolish. But what if you're nowhere even close to the limit? Then you've removed an option you had for getting out of trouble. The safest option, too. . .

Look at a horse running on a track. When it goes around a corner it leans over. Obviously. Look at an antelope running from a cheetah. As it weaves and turns it leans over. So does the cheetah as it chases its dinner. Look at a human athlete on a track event. They lean going around corners too. What's the point of these rather obvious observations? It's because if you look more closely you'll see that all those creatures in their different environments lean at pretty much the same angle. And that angle is 34°. We all have a built in inclinometer, and it says that if we lean over at more than 34° we will fall down. Of course that was true when we didn't have radial tyres, advanced chassis technology and fabulous handling motorbikes. But now, with the aforementioned motorbikes, we can safely lean to maybe 50° before it all goes wrong. Certainly we have at least 10° - or 30% - more lean than our natural instinct tells us we should have. Natural instinct is a tough thing to overcome, but if you're going to get even nearly the best out of your bike then you're going to have to try.

The rider at the other extreme is in just as much trouble. He's beaten the instinctive lean angle limit and has now got blasé about it. He thinks that he has huge reserves when in fact he's at, or very close to, the limit a lot of the time. If something happens with him, either overcooking a corner or an emergency forcing him to change line for some reason then he's really in trouble. If he tries to tighten his turn, using the reserves he thinks he has, he's going to rapidly discover just how close to the limit he is. And he's going to run out of options very quickly.

Both of these situations can be resolved. Ideally you want to get photographed at every corner so you can get a good handle on the accuracy of your estimate of, um, commitment at any point against the cold hard truth. More realistically, you should be able to get a picture at one corner. But otherwise find someone you can trust to give you an honest, accurate and impartial appraisal of how close to the limit you are at any particular point. It's an eye-opener. It's also a life saver. . .

Yep, this guy has a problem as well. Just as dangerous as the first one – he thinks he'd got plenty in reserve...

How to resolve it? Well, if you're erring on the side of caution then you just need to gradually push that little bit harder. Once you get past the psychological barrier it's actually quite easy to lean further and further, as our overconfident friend demonstrates. He on the other hand needs to slow down a little and maybe look at his cornering technique a little more closely.

Advanced techniques

These are things which you probably don't actually need but which may make your day more fun or may help you progress your riding to the next level. While none of them are huge changes to what you should already be doing, they should still be approached gently and you should build up to using them completely. Also, of course, everyone is different so what works for me may not suit you at all. Feel free to adapt and refine as you see fit.

Moving some more

If you're running out of ground clearance on corners then you can help by moving your weight some more. Nothing short of major alterations will give our bike more ground clearance, but you can turn harder for less lean angle with a bit of trickery.

Essentially you need to get your weight in towards the inside of the turn. You've started off dropping your shoulder and leaning your body inwards. Now you need to do more, and that means, quite literally, shifting your bottom. You need to slide across the seat and start to hang off a bit. There's still no need to put your knee down.

Compare this guy to the one with his knee down on page 64. Same corner, much the same speed. Who looks more in control, though?

Driving through corners

When we looked at cornering before we touched on the need to maintain a positive throttle, but we didn't really go into detail. It's important to stay on the power if you're racing because, obviously, you want to keep as much corner speed as possible and get the maximum acceleration out onto the straight. But there's more to it than that, and even on the road there are real benefits to staying on the power. The most important one is that a positive throttle keeps the rear suspension slightly loaded. An unloaded suspension assembly has a surprising amount of free play in it and that free play translates into a loose, floaty feeling, especially under cornering. Just a small amount of compression immediately tautens the whole thing up, preventing that free play and resulting in controlled, accurate feel that is exactly what you need.

As well as tightening things up in the chassis, being on a positive throttle also removes a whole load of slack in the drive train. When the throttle is closed, the whole mechanical part of your bike, from the very beginning with the throttle cable through to the final drive, is either slack or taking load in the wrong direction. So when you open up from a closed throttle you have to take up the slack in the throttle cable before you even move the carburettors or injectors. Then there is the lag before they respond. The engine itself will react to them pretty well straight away but the gearbox has to go from taking a reverse load (it's acting as a brake with a closed throttle) to a forward one and the chain has to take up the slack before it

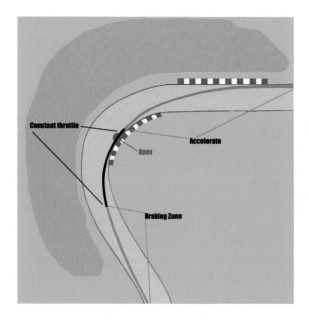

Off the brakes and onto a constant throttle to maintain your entry speed, then steadily feed in the power from the apex onwards.

can put power through to the wheel. All that translates to a tendency for snatch or jerking, making it very hard to accelerate cleanly and increasing risk of your breaking traction.

So exactly how do you drive through corners? It'll come as no surprise that, although the principle is pretty simple – get on the throttle – there are some refinements you need to add to make it work consistently and safely. First and foremost we go back to preparation and setting up for the bend. You've got the position OK, you're set up on the track and you've got the speed about right. All you need to do now is make sure you're in the right gear. In fact, you needed to do that a while ago. But that's a refinement that comes later. For now, you need to be in a gear that gives you the best engine response. You don't want to be screaming the engine because you've got nowhere to go, but at the same time you don't want to be chugging along in too high a gear. You want to be able to get decent acceleration without a particularly large handful of throttle, but at the same time you don't want to find yourself having to change up when you're still leaning over. Not a good thing.

There's something else as well, but now we're getting into some fairly serious stuff. If you're in a high gear and trying to maintain drive then you have to have a big handful of throttle. If you manage to break traction, even for a moment, then that straining engine will be free to accelerate the now spinning wheel very fast. It's quite possible that you could get your back wheel suddenly doing, say, 30mph more than you. And that means you're going to fall off unless you are far too skilled to need this book. But if you're in a lower gear, although you can put more power onto the road and in theory can provoke a slide more easily, the wheel can't be accelerated so far before the engine hits the rev limiter so you've got a chance of either catching the slide as it starts or the rev limiter stopping it from getting too lurid. It won't feel very nice and you'll probably have palpitations afterwards, but you've got a better chance of still being on the bike.

So you're in the right gear, on the right line and you're all set up ready to go. The basic routine you should expect to follow is this. As you get to the right approach speed, come off the brakes and open the throttle enough to maintain that speed. As you lean over the bike will naturally scrub speed off. Gently apply enough throttle to maintain your speed on the way in. After you've hit the apex then you can start to feed more power in, allowing the extra speed to carry you over to the outside of the track where you want to be. As you get more confident you'll find you can get on the power earlier and earlier. But take it steadily and remember that you're not racing so that ultimate speed down the straight is less important than a smooth, controlled and safe piece of fast cornering.

Complexes

On this occasion I'm not talking about you feeling as though everyone is laughing at you. We covered that earlier. No, this is about corners running into each other, be they chicanes, esses or something else. The big thing about complexes is that your entry requirements for one bend have to dictate the exit strategy for the previous one. And because, by definition, esses and chicanes have opposite direction bends flowing into each other you need to think about it a bit more than usual. Let's take a right/left complex like The Gooseneck at Cadwell Park. For now we'll forget the location and just take it as a flat track (it's actually quite steeply downhill). But anyway, if you took the first part as a single corner you'd be exiting on the left of the track around where the second corner actually starts. That, you'll hopefully recognise, is No Good. So you need to compromise on

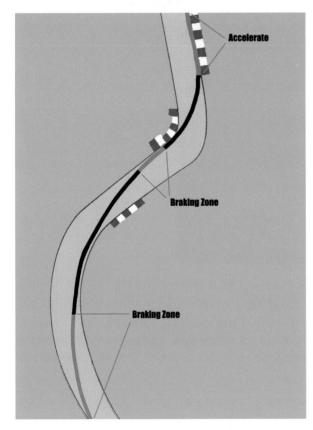

A classic entry to the first part of the complex wrecks the approach to the second part. Our hero has to brake again to turn the bike harder and can't get back on the power until he's managed to get straight again.

your first corner to nail the second. In this case it means keeping your exit speed down and staying right. Hug the inside until you get to the turn for the second corner then turn hard and treat it as usual. The key, the place so many people come unstuck, is in keeping the speed down to give yourself time and room to turn. Physically the bike will go much quicker, but you don't have the time or space to get it turned before you run out of track.

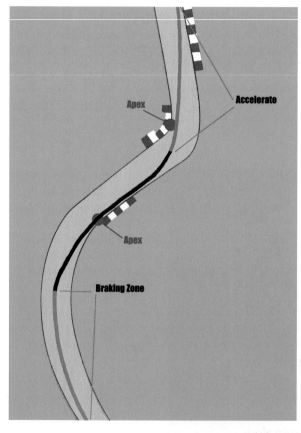

Though the first part is slower this way, that doesn't matter so much as it makes the bike easier to turn for the second part, allowing the rider to get on the power earlier and make the most of the following straight. It's much less scary, too.

Longer sets of bends, like perhaps Hall Bends, also at Cadwell, offer different challenges. Here the danger of overcooking it increases as you go through. Each bend that goes well means you should be carrying more potential exit speed which you need to manage. And the pendulum effect of going side to side can be a little peculiar at times as well as physically quite hard work.

Chicanes are nasty devices meant to slow you down. They spoil the flow of a lap but generally do make the crashes that occur slower and less injurious. Recently they've started springing up to reduce speeds before notorious accident blackspots like Devil's Elbow at Mallory Park. Actually Mallory has more chicanes than anywhere else, I think, but we'll cover that later. The principle of dealing with a chicane is the same as any other complex, but the corners are much tighter and slower. You don't need to worry about the discipline of staying slow and tight so much as the first bend will have slowed you right down anyway. No, you need to be looking especially hard at your throttle technique as chicanes are notorious places for highsides. More on those later, too. Chicanes test your braking, your ability to turn the bike hard and your throttle control. You need, normally, to lose a lot of speed before turning very hard one way then the other and getting back on the power around the second apex. Nobody is particularly fast through them, even the professionals, and plenty of people get them wrong. They bite, so build up slowly. The other thing to be aware of is that chicanes often have very tall kerbs to stop our four wheeled friends cutting the corner. Not good for your knees, so a little circumspection might be in order.

Getting your knee down

It's something that I keep getting asked about, so despite my misgivings I'll explain the mystical dark art of scraping your knees here. The trick is simple. But before I reveal it you need to understand that it really isn't necessary for you to get your knee down to go respectably quickly. Really. If you're doing it then you're doing it because it's cool. And that's OK.

To get your knee down you do not need to be going very fast. You do not need to be on a sports bike. And you do not need to be a committed nutter. I've watched a serving traffic policeman get his knee down on a Honda Goldwing at about 20mph. I didn't think he'd get it back up again but he did it. What you do need is some commitment and a supple enough physique to allow some more movement. Oh, and having knee sliders on your leathers is an excellent idea anyway, but should be considered essential for this sort of tomfoolery.

We've discussed your body language for cornering. All you need to do is make it a bit more extreme. So slide your bottom further across the seat so that you've just got one cheek still on board. Keep your body turned into the corner and stick your knee out. That, essentially, is it. Lean over and eventually your knee will touch the ground. It will feel really strange the first time, and though you'll be as excited as anything please try not to fall off through exuberance. Yes, I've seen that happen too.

Same corner as before on page 58 – it's even the same sort of bike – but a more exuberant style. Which is best? Whichever suits you...

When you are hanging off the bike that much there are several side effects. The first, biggest and most beneficial is that you have moved your centre of gravity a long way towards the inside of the turn. The direct result of this is that the bike doesn't need to be leaned over so far to turn at the same rate. So you're safer. You're potentially faster as well, because now there's lean angle to spare so you can go faster and lean more before running out of tyre or clearance. So your margin for adjustment has gone up, which again is a safety improvement. And as we've already agreed, you're looking way cooler as well.

But it's not all sweetness and light. When you first hang off the bike you'll find it odd and you may well go tense. That's only to be expected, but because you're now using the bars for support there is a real risk that your tension is going to upset the bike as well through your inadvertently adding steering input. You need to use your feet a lot for support, as well as using your outside thigh against the tank or seat. It helps, or at least I find it helps, if you keep the ball of your inside foot on the peg rather than the arch. You won't be able to reach the gearchange or brake pedal, but leaned over that far you shouldn't want to anyway. It just feels better to me.

The long and the short of it is that, at least as far as getting your knee down is concerned, provided that your knee isn't followed by the rest of your body, there isn't a right or wrong way. Just experiment to see what feels best for you.

As you get to the end of the corner you need to get back onto the seat, tuck in and get on the power, and this can get interesting. Because you're so far off the seat you'll need to use the bars to help you back up. And pulling on the outside bar will make the bike lean over further. Which can get exciting for all the wrong reasons. So if you have to use the bars for leverage to get back up, make sure it's the inside one so you can use it to get the bike straight at the same time. Or use your legs instead – a far better solution.

When it all goes wrong

Despite what you may have been told, or indeed despite the impression you may have gained from this book, falling off is neither mandatory nor even especially common. In 20 years of fairly enthusiastic and committed trackdays, for example, I have actually fallen off once. And run into the gravel once. I'm touching wood as I write this, of course. So there really is no reason for expecting anything to go wrong, but every reason for being prepared when it does.

What can go wrong

There are really only four things which can spoil your day. You can come off, you can break down, you can get sick or the weather can turn bad. If the weather turns bad then you have two choices. Pack up and go home or tough it out and ride anyway. As long as it isn't icy or flooding then the circuit will remain open regardless, and there is a huge amount of learning you can do on a wet circuit. Apart from anything else, the lack of roadside furniture and the very notable reduction in the number of riders out there makes it a spectacularly safe way to explore your, and your bike's, limits. Even if you go too far the massively reduced speeds on a wet track mean that the damage you and it suffer are likely to be extremely minor. Though it shouldn't have any bearing on things, you might also want to remember that trackday organisers do not give refunds in the event of inclement weather unless the circuit is closed by it, and even then it's at the discretion of the circuit management as to whether they refund the organiser.

Getting sick is a different kettle of fish. Assuming that it isn't a hangover, in which case sympathy will be markedly absent, you will certainly find a huge amount of support from your peers and the organisers. If you're not fit to ride then your recovery company, assuming you have one, will most likely have a clause which will recover you and your bike in the event of illness. It won't be subject to the normal track exclusions either, so you will be able to get home. Otherwise you'll probably find someone with a van or trailer who will go out of their way to help you out. It's a friendly sort of atmosphere as a rule and that sort of thing is the norm rather than the exception, especially when the problem is clearly one outside your control. But whatever happens, don't be tempted to try to carry on with a raging migraine or Galtieri's revenge or whatever. You won't be safe and you won't enjoy it, so why put yourself and your peers at risk like that?

Mechanical derangement

Motorcycles are machines, and as such they are subject to the same peculiarities as your computer, your fridge or your TV. Yes, they occasionally break down, and there are some things which make them more prone to breaking down. Top of the list is a lack of maintenance. Though machines are supposedly inanimate objects, they seem to know when they aren't being loved and cared for, and react accordingly. So make sure that your bike gets at least the minimum recommended maintenance, and ideally rather more. As an example, and I'm by no means the best person to use for this, my bike gets cleaned once a week and checked over properly at the same time. But I also do around 800 miles a week on it, so regular checks are rather important as things wear out. In fact, at that mileage I should be checking it daily, but that might be seen as obsessive...

Part of the scrutineering checks at the beginning were about maintenance and condition of your bike, so hopefully you'll be OK on that score. But I've said it before and it's worth repeating. If you want your bike to look after you and generally keep you out of trouble then you should at least extend it the same courtesy.

The other thing that tends to exacerbate the tendency for machines to fail is hard use. By that I don't mean opening the throttle harder and further than usual, braking harder and longer than usual or even riding much faster than usual. No, all these things are within the design limits of your bike and may well actually do it some good. Engines like to be run hard every now and again to give them a chance to stretch their lungs and generally get some exercise, and the rest of the bike will react much the same. No, I'm thinking of the sort of lack of mechanical sympathy that sees a rider caning the engine through the redline, slipping the clutch, ham-fistedly (ham-footedly?) booting the gears, dragging the brakes and generally abusing the machine. Best way to avoid breaking anything through such abuse is to avoid riding like that in the first place. Clumsy wheelies, or more accurately clumsy landings from wheelies, are also extraordinarily hard on the bike, as well as being frowned upon at most circuits.

Falling off

Everyone falls off at some point. Whether it's fast or slow, embarrassing or expensive, painful or pitiful, we all do it. If you can accept that as a fact and simply file it away for future reference then you should find it's one less thing to worry about.

The good thing about falling off on the track is that it's a controlled environment. That means there's nothing coming the other way, there's a distinct lack of roadside furniture to hit and things are generally arranged so that if you do find yourself yielding to the demands of Sir Isaac Newton and those pesky laws of physics you have a far better than even chance of walking away with no more than a broken motorbike. In fact most of the trackday spills I see result in the rider sitting a session out and then getting back out there with a few honourable battle scars on the bike and that's all. Obviously, the bad thing about falling off on the track is that you are probably going to be travelling rather quicker than you would be on the road, so there's rather more energy to be shed by both you and the bike. But the design of the track and runoff areas generally means that energy can be dissipated in as controlled a manner as you can reasonably expect in a, by definition, somewhat uncontrolled situation.

On a trackday there are generally three ways you can fall off. You can run wide on a corner. When you go wide you may well go into the gravel trap. You may not even actually fall off, you almost certainly won't hurt yourself and the damage to your bike should be minimal. This rates high on the embarrassment front and people will generally not feel bad about taking the mickey because it's an otherwise trivial incident. You can also find yourself going onto the grass, usually because it's a corner where there is no gravel trap or because your line was sufficiently bizarre to have missed the gravel trap completely. Falling off once you get on the grass is distinctly likely because you have very little grip and it's bumpy. Try to make sure the bike is upright, stand on the pegs and keep your weight towards the back to give the front suspension the best chance of working and use the back brake as hard as you dare. If you have to steer keep it gentle and stay off the front brake if you possibly can. Dropping the bike probably won't result in a huge amount of damage unless you're still going quite quickly and it digs in and flips, and similarly you shouldn't hurt yourself too much either.

The most common time I see people going off the track like this is on the approach to a corner. They start braking, decide they need to brake more or harder and then can't get off the brakes in time to turn in. So they try to

Not sure which is worse for this guy. The fact that he went off the track in front of his peers or the fact that I was there with a camera. At least he didn't drop it...

scrub off even more speed to make up for the late turn-in and end up going straight on. Braking, of course. It's also not uncommon for a mid-corner confidence failure to result in the rider standing the bike up and bailing out halfway round. That can get quite exciting if there are other riders in close proximity...

The second, and jointly most common, way of parting company with your machine is the lowside. The lowside gets its name from the fact that you fall off the low side of the bike when you're going round a corner as shown in the sequence opposite. There are two ways that it happens – you lose the front or you lose the back. Bet you never saw that one coming. The most common way to lowside a bike on a trackday is braking too far into a corner. You've mucked up the approach and you're carrying too much speed but you go for it anyway and either forget to get off the brakes (don't laugh – it happens more often that you might think) or decide you're still going too quickly and try to lose more speed on the approach. Either way, that tyre only has so much grip to offer and it might just give up on you. Losing the front cranked over will, no ifs or buts, put you on the ground.

The alternative is losing the back. It's less common because trackday riders tend to be more circumspect when they're winding the throttle on mid corner, but if you take a little bit too much of a liberty with your litre class sportsbike then you'll be lighting the back up in no time at all. And if you're cranked over you're either going to end up on your ear or you're far too good to be reading this. Or you're unreasonably lucky, in which case perhaps you'd like to choose my next lottery numbers?

The good thing about a lowside is that you've got very little distance to fall as you're already leaning over. The impact with the ground is a glancing one and the biggest thing you have to worry about is getting friction burns as you slide along. So relax and just go with the flow. At this point you have absolutely no control over what happens so all you can do is minimise the likelihood of hurting yourself. Relax as much as you can. Try to get your arms in. If you can fold them across your chest then that's ideal because if you start to tumble when you reach the grass or gravel then you want to avoid having limbs flailing around.

One big, big suggestion. When you've stopped sliding, lie still and count to ten before you get up. Because you want to be really, really sure that you actually have stopped. I once got off the bike at fairly high speed at Le Mans. Didn't hurt myself at all in the fall, slid along happily, bounced over the kerb, onto the grass, stopped, got up and immediately started cartwheeling. Not because I was happy to be alive but because I was still doing around 25mph at the time. And that really hurt. So take your time, do a quick systems check after you've stopped to be sure you've not hurt yourself and then think about getting up.

The third way to part company from your pride and joy is the highside. While none of the things in this section are exactly pleasurable, the highside is something you really want to avoid. Highsides always hurt, they're always immensely destructive for your bike and the chances of your continuing the day after having one are extremely slim. A highside takes place when you lose the back and then catch it, just a little bit too late. When the rear wheel starts to spin and slide out sideways the suspension gets unloaded so the shock extends. If it grips again then the shock gets compressed fast, and it kicks back. The result is that the bike gets stood up fast and the rider gets fired into the air, departing over the high side. Hence the name. Now you've got a number of problems. First of all, you're several feet in the air and travelling at some speed. Secondly, your bike is now behind you but you're going in the same direction. Thirdly, a number of Newton's laws are coming into play, and none of them are helping you. At this point, again, you have no influence over anything that happens next. All you can do is minimise the damage you suffer by spreading the impact over as

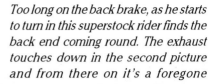

Too long on the back brake, as he starts to turn in this superstock rider finds the back end coming round. The exhaust touches down in the second picture and from there on it's a foregone conclusion. He was perfectly OK, by the way, and the bike was barely damaged.

much of your body as you can, and hope for the best. I've highsided twice. The first time was at Brands Hatch in the eighties and I ended up on the wrong side of the crash barrier. That crash finished my race career, though I didn't actually break anything. The second was at Mallory Park a couple of years ago and I had six hours or so of surgery as a direct result. So a highside isn't something to take lightly.

You'll be pleased, I hope, to learn that you can avoid a highside. Usually. Highsides only occur following a loss of grip at the back. And the only time that normally happens is through over enthusiastic application of throttle. So all you need to do is make sure that you're appropriately circumspect with your right wrist and you'll minimise the risk. The other thing, and this might be a little controversial, is to accept that if you lose the back then you're going down the track and don't try to catch it. That's pretty brave and I know I can't do it. But I also know people who can. The absolute, crucial key to not highsiding, though, is this. Don't shut the throttle if the back starts sliding. Not even a little bit. If you really must try to save it then just concentrate on getting the bike stood up but still turning. That means lots of countersteering effort and lots of weight over the inside. It's unlikely to work but if it does you'll look fabulously cool. And if it doesn't then you probably won't hurt yourself.

On a trackday it is rare to find someone falling off without warning. The reality, whether we choose to recognise it or not, is that we almost certainly got several warnings before it all went wrong. Maybe the last couple of laps felt a bit ragged. Perhaps you're not smiling anymore – you're tense and riding at the edge of your ability and way outside your comfort zone, possibly because you've got sucked into a race. Maybe you've had a slide or two, or a slight moment at a couple of points earlier on, perhaps where you've had to brake harder than you'd like or have even needed to flirt with the front brake mid corner. Or perhaps you're just starting to feel tired. Either way, the signs are there if you know where to look. So the message is simple. If you have any thought, even for a moment, that you're pushing too hard or that it's nearly time to take a rest then slip into the pits and have a break. Make up an excuse if you have to – rough running, perhaps or something in your eye – but take a timeout to regroup. The most dangerous possible phrase that can pop into your head at a time like this is "Just one more lap" because that lap is the one where it'll go wrong.

You want to know about highsides?

Here, as they say, is one I did earlier. We're at Mallory Park on a clear, sunny March morning. It's the third session of the day, I've found my rhythm, I've got some space on the track and I'm starting to turn up my pace. Everything feels great. The track is smooth and grippy where it needs to be, the occasional other riders I come up on are riding cleanly and predictably, making passing safe and straightforward. A few laps from the end of the session and I get a warning. Gerard's is wide and fast, and there isn't really a right or wrong line around it. If I'm not worried about holding a race position then I like to make it two apexes, going wide in the middle and then slicing back, getting on the power reasonably hard earlier than would otherwise be possible. Sacrificing a little mid corner speed by turning harder I get the bike stood up earlier and so I'm quicker on the exit. It also leaves more of a margin for slides and other upsets mid corner. So as I pitch into the second part of the corner I get a slide from both ends and a moment or two of wobble. Nothing too terrifying but a distinct warning that I ought to back off a bit. Perhaps the tyres are getting hot. Anyway, I decide to do a couple more laps and then pull in early. I take the next lap very gently and everything feels fine. Maybe I'm over-reacting? No matter, it's nearly the end of the session so I'll go in after this lap.

I'm approaching Gerard's at somewhere between 100mph and 120mph on my final lap. I have lots of space and the bike feels great, so I just roll off a little as I pitch in to the first part of the turn. My speed brings me out to exactly where I want to be for the next part, so I push the bars to tighten up and feel the speed scrubbing off as the bike turns. I'm almost lined up as I start to feed the power back in. The first suggestion that something is wrong is when, instead of feeling the back slide a bit as normal, I actually see the bike starting to pivot around the headstock. Yes, I'm sliding rather a lot. No problem - pull the inside bar to try and pick the bike up and roll off just a fraction - the last thing I want to do is highside, right? That didn't work. The slide is still getting bigger and I've resigned myself to a fast lowside. It'll be hot and embarrassing but I'd probably be able to ride the bike later on. Then I blew it. I listened to the arrogant little racer in the back of my head, berating me for giving up and telling me to have another go at catching it. So I did.

My next clear recollection is looking down at my bike. "This is going to hurt" was the next thought as I started to get my arms in to avoid flailing around. I'm probably six feet or so off the ground, maybe more.

Landing wasn't too nice.

Then I'm sliding along the track on my back, looking over my shoulder at my bike. I can see every detail so clearly. I can read the writing on the tyre. I can see the valves going past as the wheels turn. And I can see it all catching me up. Those wheels are doing around 130mph. And they're getting closer to me. I'm yelling "Go away, go away!" at my bike and trying to figure out where I can put my hands to push against it when we hit the grass.

I've stopped. The bike hasn't hit me.

I count to three before getting up. It's good to be sure you really have stopped.

Hurting yourself

Obviously I hope that you'll never need this bit. And statistically you're relatively unlikely to do yourself any real damage on a trackday. But the chance is always there, so you should at least know what's going to happen.

Whatever you're doing, as soon as you and your motorcycle part company at anything above a brisk walk you're going to fall over and slide around a bit. Probably that's all you'll do, but in the interests of safety, as well as to protect themselves legally, trackday organisers and/or circuit management will require you to get checked over in the medical centre if your tumble was anything other than very minor indeed. On a UK circuit you will always find marshals and a properly equipped medical centre, and the level of care you will receive at the circuit is excellent. The most likely scenario sees you taking a couple of moments laying down for a well earned rest while you get your breath back and make sure that you really have stopped while the nearest marshal makes his way over to you. If you haven't got up by the time he reaches you then you're likely to get a ride in the ambulance to the medical centre. That will probably mean a red flag for the session, but whatever you do, *don't* force yourself to get up and moving just to avoid inconveniencing anyone. That's just daft, especially if you've done yourself a mischief. Either way, whether it's in the ambulance or under your own steam, if your accident was sufficient to stop you from continuing in the session then you're going to be expected to go and get looked at in the medical centre before going out again.

The circuit medical centre has, depending on where you are, facilities ranging from those of a well equipped paramedic to something resembling a full blown trauma unit. Of course, for a trackday the super sophisticated facilities are unlikely to be manned, and your care will most probably be in the hands of a qualified and experienced paramedic. They will be able to satisfy the both of you that there is no damage or, if necessary, assess what the damage is and take appropriate action. They can stop bleeding, clean wounds up and generally make life more pleasant, but if you've done anything more than remove some skin then you will need more than they can offer and the circuit ambulance (there are usually two on call at a time so things can carry on while one is away) will take you to the nearest hospital.

Now unlike your local A&E, hospitals by race tracks have some experience of the sort of injury you're likely to have sustained, and again the treatment you'll get there will be excellent. Every case is different, of course, so it's pointless trying to tell you what will happen here. But you shouldn't be surprised if you get x-rayed, have lots of questions to answer and forms to complete and find yourself giving the same information several times. You may well also get the opportunity to experience the gentle, sympathetic, unsarcastic sense of humour for which our medical professionals are renowned the world over. That's just the way it goes – accept it and relax.

Getting your bike home

If you rode your bike to the circuit then one of the issues you're going to need to consider is how to get it, and you, home in the event of it all going horribly wrong. As I said earlier, if you get sick then that's not a problem – your recovery company should collect you without a murmur and deliver you home. But crashes and mechanical calamities are a different matter. Some recovery companies are happy to collect you from the circuit provided the bike is road legal and you weren't actually racing. Some get a bit sniffy about it. I suggest you have a chat with their customer services people if you're already a member or ask the question of the smiling salesman if they're still trying to persuade you. I can't say who does what because things change all the time and though I know my recovery people are pretty good right now, by the time you get to read this they may have been sold, had an attitude adjustment or even stopped handling bikes.

Of course, there's generally an attitude of friendly support and camaraderie at events like this, especially if they are run by novice friendly organisations, so if you've either come a cropper or your bike has undergone spontaneous self-disassembly then the likelihood of finding someone who will help you out with a lift is extremely high.

However, the bottom line is that if your recovery company won't recover you from a trackday then if anything goes awry getting home is down to you. The best option, if it's open to you, is to use a trailer or van to get there in the first place. That way as long as you're fit to drive then you're able to get everything home. Oh, and you get to use sticky as anything tyres without fear of squaring them off on the motorway, too.

And finally

When your trackday is over you'll almost certainly be exhilarated, pumped up on adrenaline and riding better than you've ever ridden before.

Stop and pause before you go out on the road for the trip home.

Check your bike is still OK – it's had a hard day and it's certainly a good idea to make sure that tyres still have tread, brake pads still have meat and so on.

Next make sure you're OK. Perhaps a short nap before you set off would be in order? You'll be pretty tired as well, especially as that adrenaline wears off. Have a coffee, maybe, and some water or juice and take the opportunity to go to the loo. It's not easy to fall asleep on a moving bike, but I'm sure it's possible and the idea of it seems like something to take the shine off an otherwise excellent day. There's no shame in being tired and admitting it, so if you need to take a rest stop on the way home then do it.

Finally, remember that the local Police know exactly what goes on at the circuit, when track days are and probably which direction the majority of riders will be headed. So ride accordingly – the circuit finishes at the end of the paddock.

Circuit guide

The circuits described in this section are shown on the map. There are other minor circuits doing occasional trackdays, but those shown here are the main venues in the country. At the end of each description there is a page on which you can make notes about your own experiences. You might, for example want to note down particular braking and turn-in points that work for you on individual corners, as well as any changes to tyre pressures and suspension settings that you've found make you more comfortable. Remember to note the weather if you're making changes – wet and dry settings will be rather different.

Brands Hatch

Ah, Britain's own cathedral of speed, the spiritual home of motorcycle racing in the UK and one of the nicest circuits ever built anywhere. There's been racing at Brands since 1924, when the circuit was a grasstrack and went the opposite direction to now. It's brilliant to ride but it's also a great place to watch, and if you're vaguely local then it's the perfect venue for popping in to see what happens before taking the plunge yourself.

On The Track

Brands has two layouts, and which one you're riding rather depends on how much you paid. Most commonly you'll be riding the short Indy circuit. You come out of the pitlane straight into the entry of the scariest corner this side of the Atlantic. Paddock Hill Bend has a virtually blind turn in point, a blind apex and an exit that has you running right out to the gravel trap as well as banging your chin on the tank as you reach the bottom of the hill. It sounds, and looks, worse than it actually is but Paddock is a truly intimidating corner that takes a long time and a lot of courage to master properly. Leaving Paddock you climb steeply back uphill to Druid's – a right hand hairpin which frequently sees overenthusiastic brakers run on into the large and accommodating gravel trap. Out of Druid's and accelerating down the hill into Graham Hill, it isn't unusual for people to realise that the left hand side of their tyre is stone cold as they slide off onto the grass on this fast, slightly downhill left hander. Then there's a short straight before the track curves left at Surtees and then swings hard right into McLaren and then Clarke Curve before opening out onto the start/finish straight. Clarke goes on forever, it's a little bumpy in places and it's not entirely unheard of for people to come a cropper trying to get on the power too hard and too early. There's not much room for that sort of tomfoolery on the exit, though the rest of the way round has acres of gravel for you to roll around in should you so desire. Some people complain that the barriers are too close to the track, but in fairness I don't believe that's really the case. Certainly it was never an issue for me racing there, and since those days things have become far tighter and the layout has been modified slightly to improve runoff. The entrance to the pitlane is on the right at the exit from Clarke.

Now as you turned off Surtees into McLaren you should have noticed a coned off section of track in front of you. If you'd paid a little more those cones wouldn't be there and you would now be riding the GP circuit.

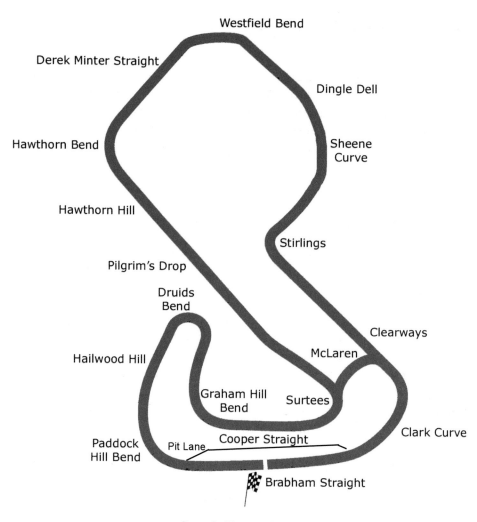

Brands Hatch Circuit

Surtees leads into the staggeringly fast Pilgrims Drop, where superbikes pull hundred yard wheelies from the sharp rise at the start of the straight. Under the bridge which still makes me flinch after hundreds of laps and into Hawthorn, a fast but quite severe right hander that catches the unwary out because it comes up so quickly. A short straight leads into another right hander at Westfield before dropping down into the infamous Dingle Dell. The next complex has been straightened out and sanitised sufficiently to give it a new name. Sheene Curve is a fast, in fact a very fast, right hander that again takes courage to master as the approach is uphill, slightly curving and essentially blind. A short straight leads into another left at Stirlings. Be careful, it's tighter than it looks. Gas it out, under the bridge and into the long right hander of Clearways. On the Indy circuit you'd now be riding around Clarke but on this it's Clearways and it starts straight after the bridge. Keeping it in line here is even more important now as the speed is so much higher after a straight. A big crash on the exit to Clearways finished my racing career, despite not actually breaking anything, but it's still a terrific corner and the circuit is definitely my favourite. I stress the number of places people get it wrong here not to scare you or put you off, but because all of them are intimately familiar to me as this is my local circuit and I've done most of the things I'm mentioning. And seen all the others.

Facilities

There is fuel on site, though it's probably cheaper to get it from one of the petrol stations outside. Food is reasonably priced from the cafe (well, sort of cafe) at the bottom of race control in the pit area and there's plenty of places to watch from if you want.

How To Get There

Brands Hatch is in Kent, just off the M20/M25 junction. Leave the M25 at Junction 3 and take the A20 signposted to West Kingsdown and, spookily enough, Brands Hatch. Watch for regular speed enforcement by police and cameras as well as the frequent and not always very clear side turnings. Brands is at the top of a hill, and the main entrance is very impressive. Follow the road around inside, go into the paddock and then do a u-turn right to take the tunnel under the track. That brings you up in the infield and it's a straight run into the pits.

Brands Hatch Circuit
Fawkham, Longfield,
Kent DA3 8NG
Tel: +44 (0)1474 872331 Fax: +44 (0)1474 874766
http://www.motorsportvision.co.uk

Brands Hatch Circuit Notes

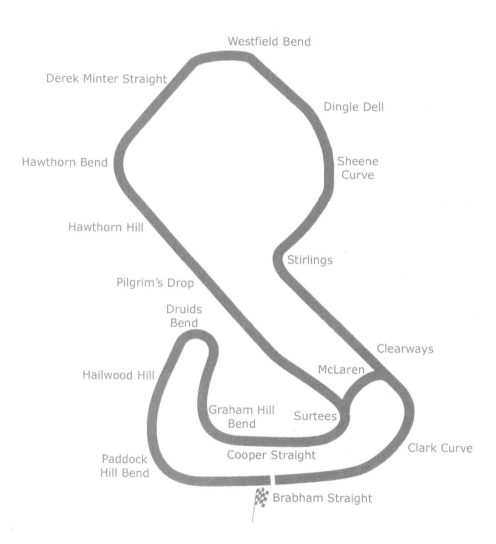

Cadwell Park

Cadwell Park in sunny Lincolnshire is one of the nicest circuits to ride anywhere. It offers everything – fast sweeping bends, tight technical bits, hills, dips, stupid chicanes and The Mountain. I'll come onto that in a minute. Cadwell was never an airfield and so isn't cursed with that same overall layout that airfield circuits have, despite their differences. It's not the safest circuit there is, though recent improvements have gone some way towards addressing that, and it isn't the easiest to learn because it's quite long. But it is incredibly satisfying to get it right and it has some of the most fun parts, as well as the most challenging, that you're likely to find. Anywhere.

On The Track

So you come out of the paddock as the pits aren't used for trackdays – be careful as it's quite steep so make sure you don't run out of leg if you have to stop – onto the beginning of Hall Bends. These have been modified over recent years, the trees have been cut back and the barrier moved a little further from the track. It doesn't look as picturesque as it used to, but you're far more likely to walk away from getting it wrong now. Hall Bends is a short right, left, right complex which rewards planning and patience. It's far too easy to charge in too quickly and find yourself progressively running out of track as you go through, so start off steadily and build your pace. The next bend, the Hairpin, is a tight, slow right hander with no runoff area whatsoever. It's not a good place to fall off - though you're unlikely to be going very fast. As is so often the case with bends like this, the two most likely scenarios are a highside when you open the throttle too hard, too early or losing the front as you realise you need to brake harder. If it's been wet then the track will be damp under the trees approaching this bend so the latter option is more likely. Both are easy enough to avoid, provided you concentrate on being smooth and build up to going fast from a steady start. The next bend, Barn, is also a tight right hander and is often regarded as one of the most dangerous in the country because the crash barrier comes back in towards the track at exactly the point that an overly aggressive rider is likely to leave the track.

It's a deceptively quick corner that needs to be treated with a lot of respect and, yet again, ridden a few times before you start to get quicker. Out onto the start/finish straight which isn't actually very long but will allow

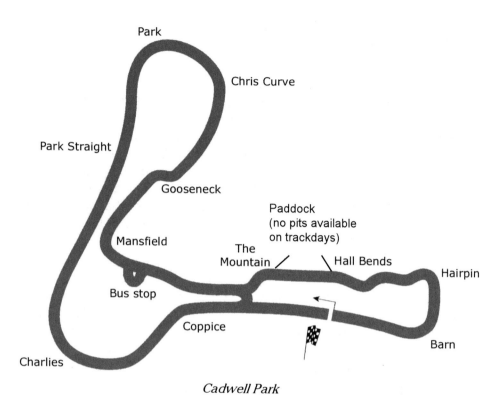

Cadwell Park

you to build a lot of speed, especially if you get a good exit from Barn. At the end of the straight the track curves left and goes uphill into Coppice. Coppice is so much faster than most people ride it, but it's a left hander and that side of your tyres won't be warm for a few laps so again a degree of circumspection is wise. Especially as the track swings out of Coppice and straight into the never ending right hander of Charlies. This is a single bend but it's so long that it works best taken as two. The track is wide but as it changes elevation and goes from uphill to downhill on the way round it can be a little daunting. Expect to have people passing you on the inside at the exit. As you start to get quicker you'll find yourself either drifting wide on the second part of the corner or having to work quite a lot harder to stay tight. There's room to do either, but beware of the track narrowing a little after the corner, making the outside edge seem to come in. You really, really don't want to hit the grass at this point. Park Straight, which comes next, isn't really a straight at all but is actually a very long left kink which dips and rises as it turns. It's very fast, and gravity helps you accelerate at the beginning and start to slow down at the end. The end of the straight is essentially blind as you crest the rise about a hundred yards before the ninety degree Park Corner. There is a huge runoff area here, so it's pretty safe, but the potential for getting it wrong at fairly high speed makes it another point you should approach with some respect. Park Corner itself is a model corner, with clear sight lines in and out, a perfectly constant radius and a nice flat surface. The only thing to be careful of is the rather high inner kerb which would hurt if you caught your knee on it. Out of Park the track carries on curving right, becoming Chris Curve. Just ride it and smile as you get quicker and quicker. There's lots of room and there are so many right lines that you can't really go too far wrong. Exiting Chris Curve you need to be over as far to the left as you can while you're scrubbing off speed for The Gooseneck, a strangely problematic little right/left downhill chicane. The secret here is to get your speed down for the first part and get yourself turned as early as possible for the second. Doing it the other way round will just give the marshals there something more to do as you run out of track on the exit. Now this next bit gets interesting. The exit of The Gooseneck is quite steeply downhill, ending in a straightforward but daunting left hander called Mansfield. Mansfield is daunting because a downhill approach puts a lot of load on the front tyre as well as on your elbows and wrists. The downhill approach also means you'll have accelerated quicker out of The Gooseneck so you've got more speed to lose. But Mansfield is straightforward because it's a simple bend with no real surprises. Again, watch that cold left side of the tyre, though. Out of Mansfield there's a very short straight which leads into a sharp and rather out of character chicane. I've rarely managed to take the same line through it twice in a session, and all I can say is that as it was designed to force you to lose a lot of speed before the next bit then it works perfectly. Leave that nasty right/left chicane and there's another very short straight leading to The Mountain. A very tight left hander leads into an equally tight right which then goes straight into about ten metres on very steep upwards hill. At the top, one of three things will happen. You may find the front goes a little light as you crest the top. You may find yourself pulling an enormous but very easy wheelie. In which case relax, it'll come down soon enough. Or you may find yourself getting totally airborne, in which case you may as well relax as you can't do anything else, but be prepared to lose quite a lot of speed when you land. After The Mountain there's another short straight before you hit the beginning of Hall Bends to do it all again.

Facilities

Although the paddock at Cadwell is small the facilities are generally quite good. The restaurant is excellent, there are plenty of good viewing areas and there is reasonably priced petrol a couple of miles down the road in Scamblesby. You should note that they may well not take plastic – they certainly didn't last time I filled up there – so make sure you have cash or a cheque book (remember them?)

How To Get There

Cadwell Park is just outside Louth in Lincolnshire, on the road to Horncastle (the A153). It's quite easy to find, being fairly well signposted, and the surrounding roads are excellent. As a result there is a regular police presence in the area so I would earnestly recommend that you confine your high speed activities to the track.

Cadwell Park Circuit
Louth,
Lincolnshire LN11 9SE
Tel: +44 (0)1507 343248
Fax: +44 (0)1507 343519
http://www.motorsportvision.co.uk

Cadwell Park Circuit Notes

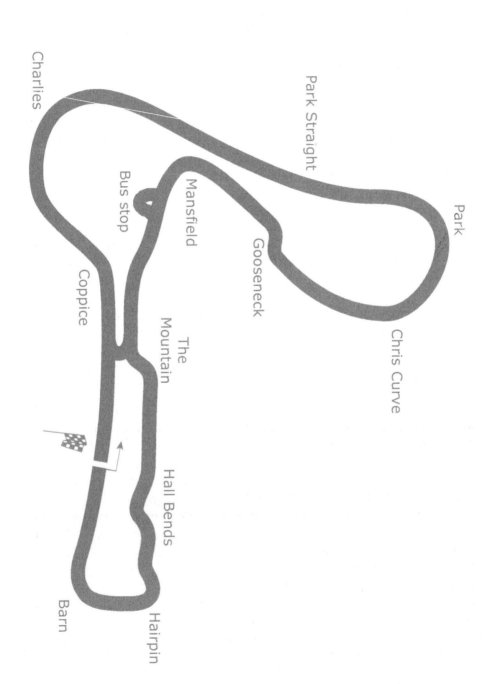

Castle Combe

Castle Combe is a beautiful little village near Chippenham in Wiltshire. Quiet, unspoiled and undeveloped, it's exactly the sort of place where gentlefolk retire and complain about noisy motorbikes. And complain they do, usually to the council. Which is why there are relatively few bike trackdays at Castle Combe circuit. The noise restrictions are draconian and rigidly enforced, and it seems that several bikes will not pass the noise tests even fresh out of the showroom. It's frustrating that people can move next to a racetrack and then enforce their will on something which has been running for years, but that's democracy for you. It isn't the fault of the circuit organisers so if you get excluded please don't take it out on them...

On the track

In many ways similar to Thruxton, Castle Combe is fast, bumpy and well surfaced. Rather than being featureless, its location on the top of a small hill means that several corners are blind. Which makes things a little more exciting. Sometimes a little more exciting than you might want it to be. Being the site of a wartime airfield, the circuit follows very much the same overall shape as you'll see if you look at the perimeter track of airfields everywhere, modified slightly with the occasional chicane. Oh, and the domed shape meant the underpowered, overloaded aircraft at the time had a bit of a bump to help them get airborne halfway down the runway.

Should you find yourself at Castle Combe then on leaving the pits you will join the track on the exit of a slight left turn, and you'll be faced with a gently uphill straight with an interesting left kink leading straight into the fastish right hander of Quarry Corner. Following on from Quarry is a short straight with a very tight chicane, The Esses, halfway along it, designed to slow you down before the entry to the next fast right hander. A gently curving but very fast semi straight, appropriately named Hammerdown, leads into another typically constant radius fast right hander, Tower Corner. Tower is followed by a tight right/left chicane called Bobbies, breaking up what would otherwise be a scarily fast, very gently curved straight. At the end of this straight is a long right hander, liberally decorated with white paint as the starting grid actually goes around it. This is Camp Corner, named presumably for the military accommodation that used to be nearby rather than the deportment of the gentlemen who stood there watching. The pitlane entry is on the left as you approach this corner, by the way.

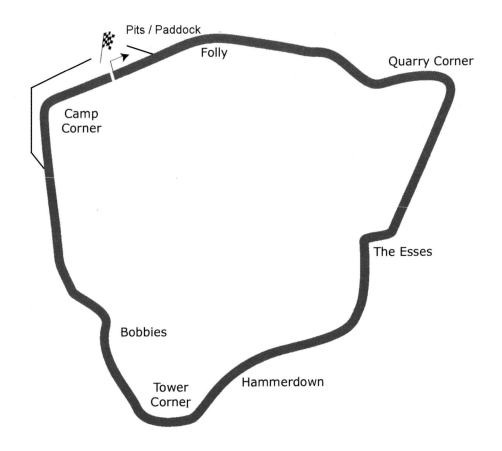

Castle Combe Circuit

It's worth bearing in mind that, though it's a very friendly and not very complicated circuit, there is precious little in the way of runoff, and there are several barriers ever so close to the edge of the track. So build up gently. It's a green and pleasant area, which does rather suggest a tendency towards rain as well. Certainly my own experience of the place does rather reinforce that suggestion.

Facilities

There is fuel just outside the circuit and there is pretty good catering on site. Well, it was good last time I was there anyway.

How to get there

Castle Combe is off the A420, just West of Chippenham in Wiltshire. That's Junction 17 of the M4 if you're coming from almost anywhere in the UK. It's clearly enough signposted from the main road, and the circuit is quite easy to spot. The approach road can be a little iffy so to avoid unpleasantness, as well as keeping the locals happier, it's probably a good idea to keep your speed down along there.

Castle Combe Circuit
Castle Combe, Chippenham
Wiltshire, SN14 7EY
Tel: +44 (0)1249 782417/782929 Fax: +44 (0)1249 782392
www.castlecombecircuit.co.uk

Castle Combe Circuit Notes

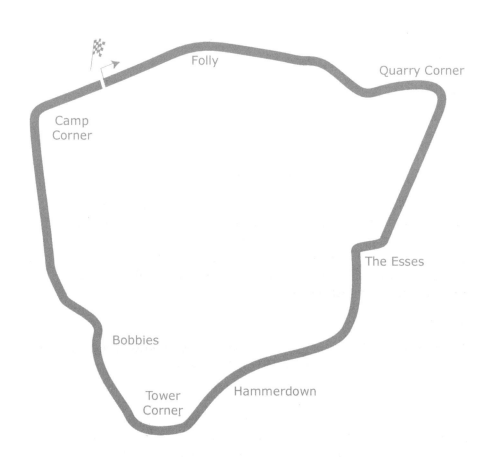

Donington Park

Ah, Donington. The home of the *real* British Grand Prix, the place where Valentino Rossi and his chums defy physics every year, where Nori Haga came to his first European race and pasted everyone in the snow, the place where World Superbikes was born. Donington has loads of bike history and is one of the most exciting places there is to ride. It flows beautifully, it has just about every type of corner going, it has elevation changes and it has huge runoff everywhere so you've got a very good chance of getting away with any minor mistakes. In fact the only bad thing about Donington is a bizarre fixation with noise. It's bizarre because Donington Park circuit is right next to Castle Donington, also known as East Midlands Airport. And I've yet to find a motorbike that's louder than a commercial airliner. But hey – as usual the rules are imposed on the circuit by the local council without any thought for logic. So though there are noisy sessions, the majority of trackdays at Donington are for road silenced machinery only. So if your bike doesn't fit that description I'd suggest you get on the phone to the organiser before you book.

On The Track

Donington may be exciting and it may well flow beautifully. But it isn't an easy circuit to ride well and it isn't a particularly easy circuit to ride fast. In several seasons of racing I never actually finished a race at Donington, and have probably got intimate knowledge of every single gravel trap around the place. But it says something for the design of the circuit that, despite getting off probably twenty different race bikes around there I never once hurt myself.

Leaving the pitlane you are immediately at the entrance to Redgate, the first turn on the circuit. This ninety degree right hander is deceptive in that it goes on longer than at first appears, a neat trick for a corner which is otherwise very straightforward. A very, very short straight leads into the next right hander of Hollywood. Now things start to get interesting here as the track drops away down one of the most famous pieces of tarmac in the racing world. Craner Curves is a daunting combination of actually quite gentle bends made far more difficult by the steep downhill gradient that tries to throw you offline. It's very, very fast down here, but I would urge you to build up to it gently. The key is to give yourself as much room as possible by making the turns wide and nailing the apexes properly. At the bottom of Craner is the Old Hairpin. Not really a hairpin at all, this right hander is faster than it looks and is a favourite overtaking place. But it's

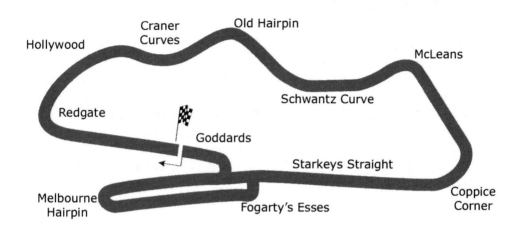

Donnington Park Circuit

also popular for falling off as you're carrying a lot of speed from Craner and it isn't *that* fast. A long, gentle left curve makes up Starkey's Bridge. There is a bridge across the track here, as well as the famous though rather forlorn looking Spitfire on the banking to your right (no, this isn't the best time to be looking at it) and the track swings in an ever tightening left hander, gently uphill through Schwantz Curve into the fast right hander of McLeans. Now you've got a few seconds breathing space as the track goes straight for a bit, uphill into probably the hardest bend on the circuit. Coppice has the double delights of a virtually blind entry and a pretty major bump halfway round. It's a seemingly endless right hander and the second part is crucial as it leads out onto the main Starkeys Straight. Falling off at Coppice, either losing the front or overpowering the rear, is a very common occurrence. Happily the gravel trap is truly vast but it's a fast place to go seeing how effective it is, so as with many other places here circumspection is probably the best approach. Starkeys Straight is, at least, straight and has no complications. The crest under the bridge is a common place for involuntary wheelies and the photographers often hang around there, but things will, or should, be well under control before you need to worry about braking or turning. Most trackdays use the National Circuit at Donington, so at the end of Starkeys Straight you'll be hauling hard on the brakes to turn right and then left into the chicane at Goddard's, exiting onto the pit straight for another lap. There's a bit of a crest halfway round which can make things a little exciting, so again take your time getting used to things. If you and the organiser have paid more then you may be using the GP circuit, in which case you'll be braking hard at the end of the straight and turning left into the Foggy Esses and out onto the Melbourne Loop. It's got better recently, but this section is notoriously slippery in the wet as for some reason a lot of vented jet fuel seems to end up on it. Anyway, the loop is two straights with a hairpin at one end. This one is a real hairpin too, and you're going into it downhill. So it's easy to run wide and onto the grass, as well as being common to get torpedoed by one of your peers. Exiting the Hairpin you come back up over the crest and are hard on the brakes for the off camber, downhill left of Goddard's, exiting onto the pit straight as before.

Facilities

It should come as no surprise to hear that facilities at Donington are excellent. There is good on-site catering, there is fuel on site and the paddock and pit areas are very nice indeed. There are also plenty of good viewing areas, and if you get a chance then the walk across the infield (there is a tunnel) to see Craner Curves really puts everything into perspective.

How To Get There

Donington Park is in Derbyshire, North of Birmingham, but is easily reachable from the M1 and M6 on one side and the M42, M40 and M5 on the other. Needless to say it is well signposted from everywhere, but if you're struggling then heading for East Midlands Airport will get you in the right area. Head for the Paddock and VIP entrance rather than the usual main entrance and just go across the roundabout, through the barrier and straight into the paddock area.

Donington Park Grand Prix Circuit
Castle Donington
Derby, DE74 2RP
Tel: + 44 (0) 1332 810 048 Fax:+ 44 (0) 1332 850 422
http://www.donington-park.co.uk

Donnington Park Circuit Notes

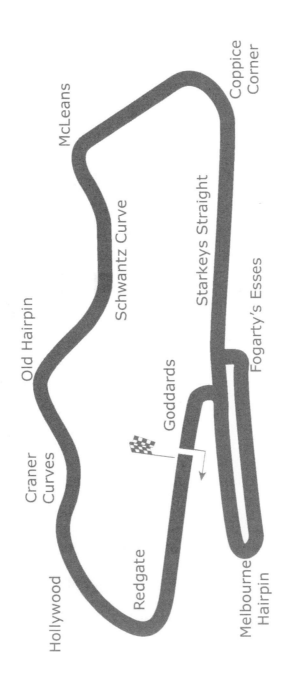

Knockhill

Up in the wilds of Fife is a shining example of what can be achieved with a bit of determination and quite a lot of money. Knockhill circuit was built from scratch by a chap who thought Scotland needed a permanent race circuit and who thought he was the man to do it. After a slightly faltering start, Knockhill was born and has gradually matured. The previously diabolical facilities have been massively improved, the paddock no longer has puddles large enough to hide Nessie and the whole place has taken on an air of a professional circuit.

On The Track

It's a short lap at just over a mile and the track is quite narrow. But drainage is good and the whole track is on a slope, so when it rains the surface dries out again quite quickly, And the surface is generally quite grippy as well.

You come out of the pitlane onto the main straight, heading downhill. There's a right/left combination ahead of you called Duffus Dip. The first apex is blind over the brow as the dip gets steeper, and that brow, allied to the right hand corner, makes this a favourite spot for losing the front if you're overenthusiastic. You can go quicker than you'd expect, but build up to it. Bear in mind that, as there's a left hander coming right up, you really need to be using just half the track to avoid getting completely off line. Only use half the track exiting the left as well or you'll seriously cramp your style for the upcoming right at McIntyre. This is a ninety degree right hander which again drops away steeply. If it's wet then you should be rather careful here as it's not unheard of for there to be standing, or rather flowing, water here. Turn earlier than you might normally expect, but watch for the raised kerb on the apex which could be rather unpleasant to hit with your knee or footpeg. You've got a short run from here to the next corner, another complex. Butchers and Glenvarigill. Butchers is a gentle right at the bottom of the hill, but there's a bit more of a drop before it levels out, so again watch that front. It's blind through here too, so again build up to getting fast. The next part is uphill. There's a severe brow almost on the apex of the left hander before swinging right through the chicane at Glenvarigill. You just might take off there – you'll almost certainly wheelie – so be prepared. Grip isn't as fantastic as it might be on the exit, so be a little cautious with the throttle. A short fast straight brings you to the next challenge, Clark. As is the norm around here, Clark is a blind corner. The approach is slightly uphill, which helps you get some speed off as well as

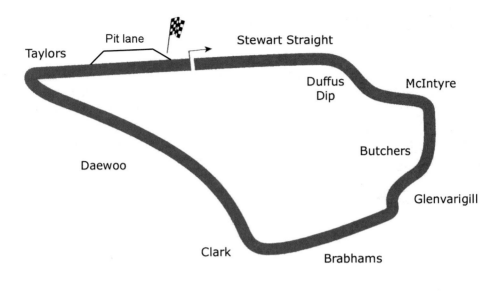

Knockhill Circuit

working to give you a better camber. There's another brow just about dead on the apex , just to make things interesting. The long gentle left hander of Daewoo Bend leads slightly uphill to the steeply uphill Taylor's – a right hand hairpin back onto the start straight. As it's a hairpin, there isn't really a right or wrong line. Well, if you crash then the line may have needed improvement. Other than that, take your own way around. Ideally, though, you should turn in to a hairpin late and apex late. Watch for highsides on the exit, as well as the ever present risk of getting torpedoed by one of your session mates.

Facilities

Facilities remain sparse though miles better than before. It's friendly, there's usually fuel on site and you should be able to get food too. Take your wet weather gear because it rains there quite a lot.

How To Get There

Knockhill is just North of Dunfirmline on the A823 in Fife, Scotland.

Knockhill Racing Circuit
Dunfermline, Fife KY12 9TF
Tel: +44 (0)1383 723337 Fax: +44 (0)1383 620167

Knockhill Circuit Notes

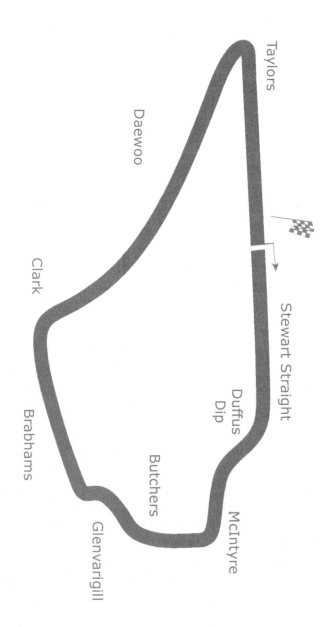

Lydden

I don't remember racing at Lydden at all, though I know I must have done so at some time. So for the sake of having something useful here rather than just filling the space, club racer Tim 'Chunky' Churchill has been kind enough to give us his view.

On The Track

Set in a bowl shaped valley it offers a chance to cut your teeth in the world of track riding without having the added hassle of a circuit that's overly complicated to learn simply where it goes. That isn't to say that's its boring, far from it.

The circuit is getting pretty old now so the surface is rather patchy in places but don't let that put you off as the patches tend to be away from where you need to be.

Entering the circuit from the pit area you will immediately be faced with an uphill approach to Paddock Bend. For the time being I'll not worry about describing it as the pits are so close to it you won't be going fast enough for it to constitute a corner.

After you negotiate Paddock from the pits you head downhill through a slight left kink into Pilgrims. You will want to keep to the left through the kink to help with your line into Pilgrims. Pilgrims is at the bottom of the hill and you should look to apex just as the track starts to rise. Start to drift out right to around the middle of the track but no further than that as you need to turn back the inside to apex for Chessons Drift. Chessons Drift is effectively a ninety degree long sweeping right hander that is apexed just after the crest of the hill allowing you to drift really wide, but in reality Pilgrims and 'The Drift' become one full 180deg, sweeping double apex, right hander. As you drift wide down the Dover Slope to Devils Elbow you need to try and get to the right as soon as you can to allow as straight an approach as is possible to Devils Elbow.

Devils Elbow is a relatively straight forward 100^0 lefthander but with it being the only left hander on the circuit your tyres will struggle to warm up for the start of a session so take care when getting on the power.

As you exit Devils Elbow you need to again swap sides of the track for North Bend. North Bend is a straightforward 180^0 hairpin, but with an

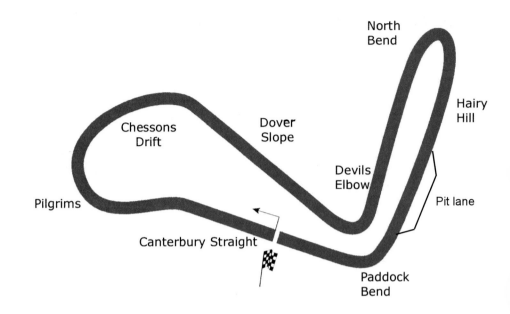

Lydden Hill Circuit

uphill approach you can use gravity to help you slow down, allowing you to brake later than you would normally anticipate. Exiting North Bend you will find yourself heading downhill towards the final corner at Paddock. Approaching Paddock Bend you are going downhill so braking will again be affected, but as a 90⁰ bend it is relatively straightforward to negotiate. Your turn in should be nice and late to give you maximum drive down the to the start finish line.

And that's it. Lydden hill in a nutshell. I have not included any information regarding gears or speeds as lets face it everyone is different.

How to Get there
Lydden Hill is located in Kent just off the A20, not a million miles from Dover.

Lydden Race Circuit
Wootton, Canterbury
Kent CT4 6RX
Tel: +44 (0)1304 830557 Fax: +44 (0)1304 831715
http://www.lyddenracecircuit.co.uk

Lydden Hill Circuit Notes

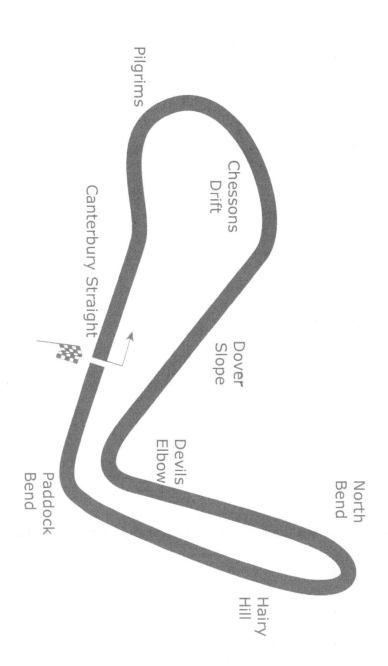

Mallory Park

Mallory Park in Leicestershire is commonly referred to as the friendly circuit, and not without reason. As well as having some of the nicest staff anywhere I've ever visited, it's in a nice location, is easy to get to and has probably the most novice friendly layout of any circuit anywhere. Mallory is exceptionally easy to learn and to ride reasonably quickly, it is blessed with a bend guaranteed to help you get your knee down if that's what you want and a great combination of fast and slow stuff. Despite having a couple of rather intrusive chicanes added in recent years, the essential character of the circuit has remained unchanged. It's also generally pretty safe. Mallory remains one of my favourite circuits to ride despite being the venue of one of my biggest, at least in terms of injury, track crashes.

On The Track

Leaving the pitlane you are immediately confronted with the entrance to Gerard's. Gerard's is a 190° right hander. The track is wide and well surfaced, there isn't really a right or wrong line and it's just lovely. If you really want to get your knee down then this is the place to learn. And if you just want to go round corners fast then it doesn't get much better than this either. In the last couple of years a new chicane has been added at the end of Gerard's in an attempt to slow things down. It worked, and if your organiser is using it (it's not compulsory) then two thirds of the way around you'll need to get the bike stood up, almost stop and take a vicious right/left/right through Charlies. Personally I think it spoils the flow, but I can understand the reasoning behind it. Leaving either Gerard's or Charlies, you come out onto the Stebbe Straight. This used to be rather a lot longer, but again as a safety measure a new chicane was added a few years ago. Edwinas forces you to again slow right down for a sharp left/right flick that sees far too many highsides on the exit as well as a fair few people losing the front or running straight on on the way in. Fortunately the old track is still there so there is an escape route if it all goes wrong on the approach, but heavy handed throttle applications on the exit will dump you on your ear. Edwinas has rather straightened out the approach to the old Esses, which is ironic as the objective was to slow bikes down there. Now you can stay flat out as you swing left through the Esses before braking as hard as you possibly can for Shaws, the right hand hairpin. There are lots of lines through here, some defensive and some faster, and the biggest danger is getting rammed by someone trying to go down the inside (which isn't the fastest way) or having to brake to avoid someone running out of track.

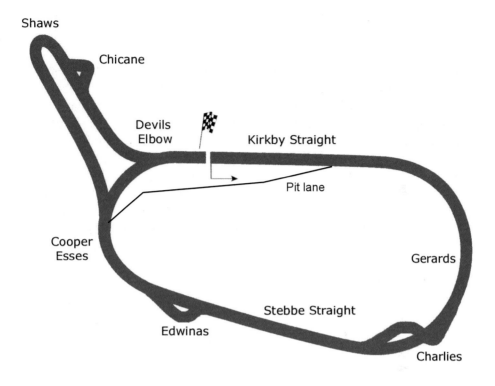

Shaws

Chicane

Devils
Elbow

Kirkby Straight

Pit lane

Cooper
Esses

Gerards

Stebbe Straight

Edwinas

Charlies

Mallory Park Circuit

It's a good idea to allow yourself some space on the way in, and the preceding section of track gives you room to let people go, or consolidate your lead over the following group, before the upcoming tight bits. As you clear Shaws, don't be too keen on the throttle as the daddy of all chicanes is waiting for you. The Chicane also known as The Bus Stop is a very tight left/right/left with no margin whatsoever to run on or cut the corner. Mercifully, coming straight after the Hairpin you'll be approaching it slowly. It was the first chicane installed at Mallory, and is designed solely and simply to slow bikes down as they approach the next corner, the fast, fearsome and scarily short of runoff, Devil's Elbow. Leaving this very high speed left hander you find yourself back on the start/finish straight powering down to Gerard's for another go.

Facilities

Facilities do leave something to be desired in the paddock area. It's gravel and, though quite solid enough to stand a bike on, it gets a bit icky when it rains. And there is simply outstanding on-site and inexpensive catering. On site fuel is available though, as usual, you'll find it cheaper elsewhere.

How to get there

Mallory is centrally located in England, near Leicester. It is easily accessible, and clearly signposted, from the M1 Junction 21, from the M6/M69 and from the M5/M42 via the A5. The nearest large town is Hinckley though the circuit is actually located in the village of Kirkby Mallory. There is only one entrance to the circuit, so follow directions from the marshalls once you get there. You will need to cross the track to reach the paddock, so arriving late will cause you a delay while you wait for the session to finish.

Mallory Park Circuit
Kirkby Mallory, Leicestershire, LE9 7QE
Tel: +44 (0)1455 842931/2/3 Fax: +44 (0)1455 848289
http://www.mallorypark.co.uk

Mallory Park Circuit Notes

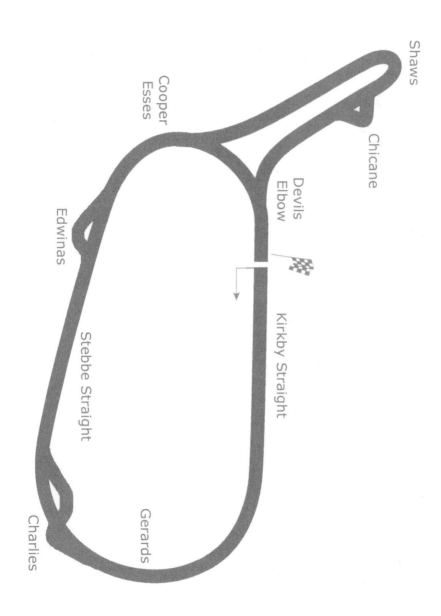

Oulton Park

Oulton Park in Cheshire is regarded by many as the most picturesque circuit in the country. Certainly it is attractive with its lake and woods, and it's a rider's favourite as well, combining intensely technical sections with very fast bits.

On The Track

Now it's quite a while since I've been there, so this lap guide was written by Superstock racer Gareth Hankinson. Look at it as a racer's viewpoint rather than using it as gospel for your trackday experience...

Along the start finish straight you are flat out in 5th gear at about 155mph, dropping down into 3rd for the first right hand corner, Old Hall. This is taken at roughly 100mph and is very bumpy which upsets the bike, you have to be careful getting on the power as the bike skips and tries to wheelie. You also need to make sure you don't run wide onto the grass at the exit. Next up its Cascades. Try to keep a tight line on the way in. It's a blind approach in 5th gear at about 150mph. It's important to get a good drive out of here, getting on the power really early, and to get well tucked in for the straight. Again that's flat out in 5th, roughly reaching a top speed of about 170mph then back down a gear into 4th for the frighteningly quick left hander of Island Bend, taken at about 115mph. As you approach Shell Oils right hander there are a few bumps which make the rear go very light so be careful and try to brake in a straight line. Try not to brake too hard as the hairpin is much faster than it looks because of its camber. Ideally it's taken in 2nd at around 70mph. Accelerate very hard out of there, the banking allows you to do this but make sure you have stood the bike up for the fast right towards Britten's. This is an unusual chicane as it's actually a very fast place taken in 2nd at about 75mph. As you come out of there short shift up Hill Top to try and keep the front wheel down, again the bike becomes very lively here and is a handful. Next up its very hard braking for Hizzy's Chicane, back to 2nd gear for the right 60mph up to 3rd on the way out about 90mph hold it briefly until you see the apex then flat out up Clay Hill which is taken in 5th gear, roughly 120mph. This is one of the most difficult parts of the track, it's very fast, very steep and very narrow. The barriers are also very close which can be scary at times especially in the wet so do not miss the apex on the right or you risk having a big one.

Next up it's Druids which is a double apex right taken in 3rd gear at roughly 100mph. There is a big bump on the exit of Druids and the bike goes very light and will want to wheelie. The next straight is like a roller-coaster all the way to Lodge where you can brake very late, remembering to defend

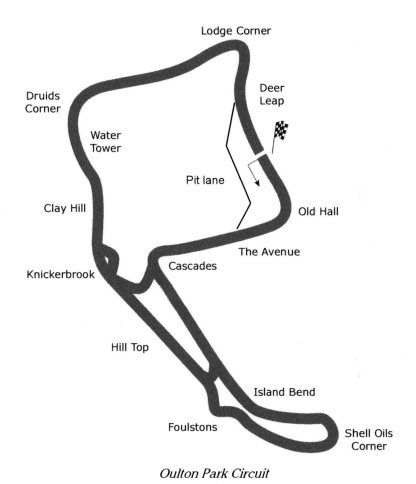

Oulton Park Circuit

your line as this is where a lot of passes will happen. Back to 2nd for Lodge at 80mph then through Deer Leap which goes downhill then straight back up again. The front goes light here, sometimes you need to slightly close the throttle to stop you running out towards the barriers on the start finish line for another lap!

How to Get There

Oulton Park is situated just off the A49 in Cheshire, near Tarporley in the village of Little Budworth. It is quite well signposted after you come off the motorway.

Oulton Park Circuit
Little Budworth, Tarporley,
Cheshire CW6 9BW
Tel: +44 (0)1829 760301 Fax: +44 (0)1829 760378
http://www.motorsportvision.co.uk

Oulton Park Circuit Notes

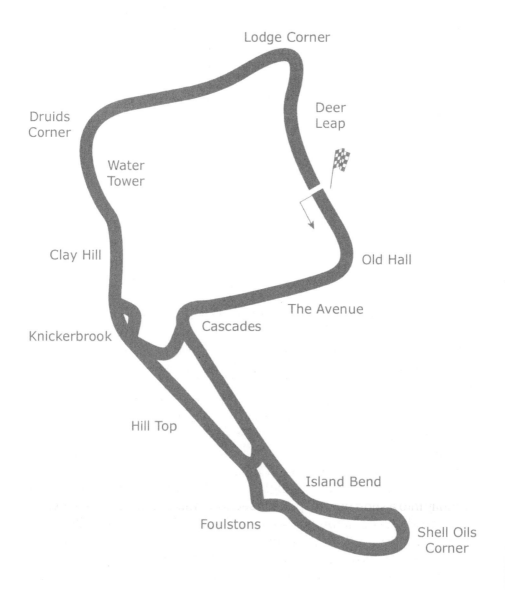

Rockingham

The newest proper racetrack in the UK, Rockingham is a purpose built circuit near Corby in Northants. Originally conceived for NASCAR style racing, the large banked oval is impressive in itself though appallingly bike unfriendly. What is far more impressive is the technically challenging and varied infield circuit which is usually used for bike trackdays. There is another layout which incorporates some of the banking but this is usually reserved for competitive meetings. In recent years, Rockingham's popularity seems to have waned a little with trackday organisers, which is a shame as it's an interesting, grippy and relatively safe circuit which is also blessed by being far enough from anywhere in particular to be relatively relaxed with their noise restrictions.

On The Track

Joining the circuit from the enormous and well surfaced pit area involves crossing the paddock – no hardship as again it is vast and properly surfaced – because the main pit exit leads onto the banked section. Coming out onto the main straight you have a short run up to the First Corner, a ninety degree right hander which, though quite straightforward to take sees an undue amount of gravel trap action. Perhaps it's because this is the only true straight on the circuit, or perhaps it's because the corner is so simple. Either way, going straight on under braking or running wide on the exit are both popular ways of enjoying the large gravel trap on this corner. Assuming that you have remained upright, though, there is a very short straight leading into a the Little Chicane which can be taken on most road bikes without really slowing down at all. A slight drop leads into the next right hander, which opens up nicely into the back straight. This isn't really straight at all, comprising as it does a long, fast, right hand curve and culminating in a scarily fast proper right hand bend. Another short straight ends in a second ninety degree right hander (Sharp Right), this one leading instantly into a short but steep uphill section similar to, but not as ferocious as, Cadwell Park's mountain section. Clearing the top of the hill you go immediately into a flowing section of right and left hand bends, mainly leading straight into each other and finishing up with a long, fast left hander that allows you, should you be so inclined, to wear away your left knee slider as well as the right one – a rare treat in this country. A very short straight leads into the right hand Hairpin which in turn leads you back onto the main straight and another lap.

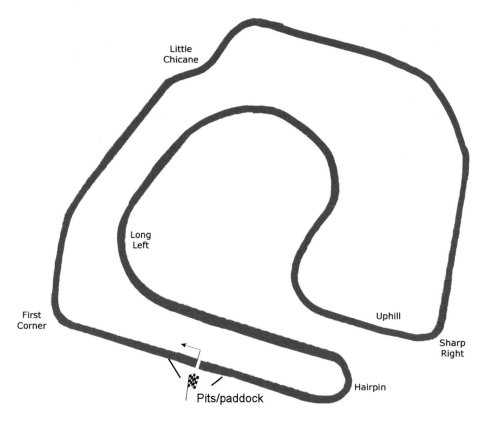

Rockingham Circuit

Facilities

Being new but geared to car racing more than bikes, Rockingham's facilities are excellent in terms of pits and paddock. But because of the sheer size of the place it's a long way to any fixed catering facilities. Now last time I was there we were lucky enough to have an excellent mobile caterer – ideal if you happen to like traditional trackside fare like egg and bacon sandwiches, sausages and so on but neither sophisticated nor veggie friendly if either of those are more your bag. Surprisingly, there was no fuel available on site either, though the nearest petrol station is just a short ride away.

How To Get There

Being modern and purpose built, Rockingham is quite easy to get to. It's just North of Corby, about ten miles off the A14 – that main trunk road between the M11 and the rest of the world – and provided you remember that, at the time of writing, there are almost as many speed cameras as people in Northamptonshire, the journey there should be quite simple. The main entrance takes you straight in, and you follow the signs to take a large tunnel under the track and into the paddock area.

Rockingham Motor Speedway
Mitchell Road, Corby
Northamptonshire NN17 5AF
Tel: +44 (0)1536 500500 Fax: +44 (0)1536 500555
Website: www.rockingham.co.uk

Rockingham Circuit Notes

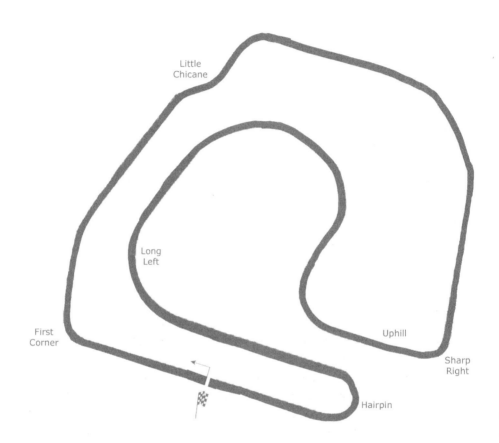

Silverstone

The home of the British Grand Prix and joint claimant to the title of the home of British Motorsport, Silverstone is a former wartime airfield (now there's a surprise). It is rather open, somewhat flat and just a little featureless. There are those who feel that when it comes to bikes it's just a little too open and, to be brutally honest, boring. It's also surprisingly difficult to learn as there is a slight lack of reference points for braking and turn in points and the track is so wide that accuracy often suffers. Silverstone has a number of circuit layouts, but virtually all bike events use the National circuit which cuts out Hangar Straight and Stowe Corner but frequently (though not always) adds a rather funky chicane to the start of the pit straight. If you watch the racing on TV then you should be aware that this is not the layout used in Superbikes – they use the International Circuit which is a little longer and more interesting. There are not very many bike trackdays at Silverstone, possibly partly because of the price but mainly because of the amount of four wheel testing and development that goes on.

On The Track

You exit the pitlane onto the end of the start/finish straight, just before turning into the long right hander at Copse. A surprisingly long, slightly uphill straight leads into the complex at Maggots, which looks far less of a complex on paper than it actually is when approached at speed. Especially as it seems to come out of nowhere. This complex ends in the sharp right hander of Becketts, which in turn flows straight into a long, gentle, multi-apexed left curve. A short straight is followed by the right hand hairpin of Abbey, a favourite outbraking place in racing and a favourite running out of track place on trackdays. Another gentle left and another short straight, dropping under the bridge, brings you up to the fast, slightly uphill Bridge corner. Carry on uphill for a short distance and then peel left into Priory. Again the blind entry at the crest of a rise makes this a favourite gravel surfing venue for pro and amateur alike. A very short straight leads into the never ending left hander of Brooklands, which in turn leads straight into the slow right hander of Luffield. Now you may have had a short straight in there, in which case Luffield opens up into the gentle and very fast right of Woodcote before coming onto the start/finish straight for another lap. But bikes usually get turned earlier, making Luffield flow straight out of the end of Brooklands and lead into a sharp and notoriously unforgiving left/right chicane. The good news is that if you come in too

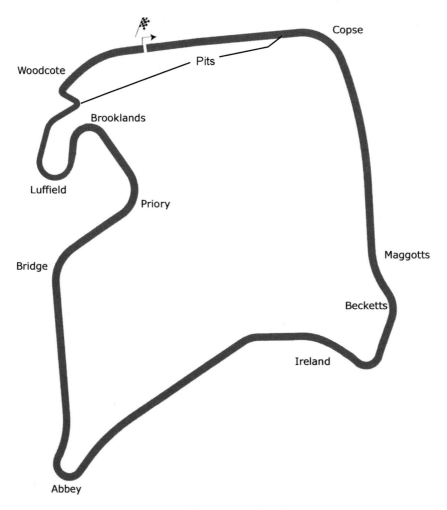

Silverstone Circuit

hot you can go straight on into the pitlane and claim you meant to all along. The bad news is that some seriously talented racers have come a cropper in this chicane, which was designed to slow bikes down along the straight in an attempt to make it all a bit safer.

Facilities

Silverstone has excellent and reasonably priced catering facilities adjacent to the paddock. There is supposed to be fuel on site, though I have never managed to find it, but there is also an offsite petrol station in either direction on the main road. The paddock is well surfaced and level, and pit boxes, as you'd expect, are large, plentiful and beautifully maintained.

How To Get There

Silverstone is on the borders of Northampton, Buckingham and Oxfordshire and is spectacularly easy to get to. The A43 is a dual carriageway linking the M40 and the M1, and there is a four lane access road from the A43 to the circuit. Yes, four lanes. One thing you won't be doing is sitting in a queue to get into your trackday. Once you're in the circuit, go over the bridge and follow the signs to the paddock.

Silverstone Circuit
Northamptonshire NN12 8TN
Tel: +_44 (0)8704 588 200 Fax: +44 (0)8704 588 250
http://www.silverstone.co.uk

Silverstone Circuit Notes

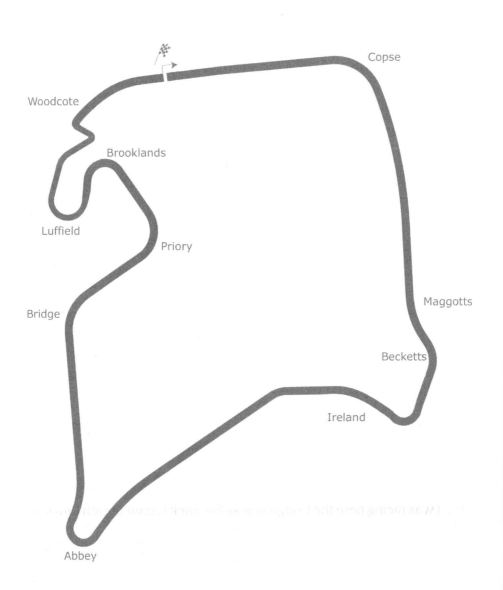

Snetterton

A former bomber base, Snetterton in Norfolk used to have the fastest, hairiest bend in the country as well as some of the longest, fastest straights. Though safety fears have sanitised it a little, Snetterton remains a challenge to ride well despite being fairly straightforward and easy to learn. Back in the old days, the circuit was nearly twice the length it is now, with four

long, flat out straights. The old section was abandoned, allegedly, when a racing car left the track and went through the hedge onto the main road. That may be a urban legend but it's a funny picture nonetheless. There is also a Sunday market held on that part now, which helps to pay for the circuit upkeep while adding to raceday traffic. But that won't worry you.

On The Track

Coming out of the pits you'll be about two thirds of the way down the main straight, heading into the first right hander at Riches. The cabbage field on the outside is legendary for having as many motorcycle and car parts planted in it as vegetables, but at least there's plenty of runoff before you get there. It's a fast bend but, like most others here, takes some building up to as well as some courage before you can really take it properly. A very short straight takes you to Sears, another ninety degree right hander which is rather sharper than Riches. There's a wide concrete area on the exit that you can drift out onto if you want to. Just take it easy until you know that it's not covered in gravel and other stuff, because that's not unheard of. Nor is it unheard of for people to open the throttle too hard or too early and launch themselves over the highside. I'd urge you not to join them – you'll be going plenty fast enough at the other end of the straight, no matter how late you decide to nail it. Revett Straight is long, fast, flat and, surprisingly enough, straight. If you want to stretch your bike's legs then this is a good place to do it. Full blown superbike racers hit 200mph here, so go for it. At the end of Revett you encounter The Esses. Now when I was racing here the bridge across the track forced the left turn into the Esses and gave you a fairly bleak choice – get turned or hit the base of the bridge. It was also an extremely tight turn needing some major deceleration. One of the more welcome safety improvements was the moving of the bridge away from there and a serious relaxing of the bends. In fact, the bridge was moved and the bends was moved too, shortening the straight by a hundred metres or so. As a result, you can turn into the left very fast indeed and there's still time to sit up and shed a lot of speed for the rather tighter second part of the complex. A very short straight takes you into the right hand bend of The Bomb Hole, which as the name

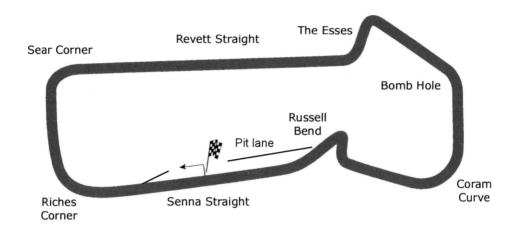

Snetterton Circuit

suggests is in something of a dip. It's a good test of your suspension and setup if you're planning on taking it fast. Leaving the Bomb Hole you're almost immediately turning right again into Coram Curve, which used to be the fastest and scariest turn on the calendar. As it is, you're cranked over accelerating round this never ending bend which opens out, gets faster and then suddenly turns into a chicane. Russells used to be a flat out left hander onto the start/finish straight but that was so appallingly dangerous that it was replaced by a tight chicane instead. So hard right then left and back onto the straight for another lap. Visibility into Russells is good and it's not as daunting as it sounds. But the left hand side of your tyres won't be very warm so you'll need to be a little circumspect about getting the power on too hard. Remember that Mr Highside just loves chicanes.

Facilities
Facilities at Snetterton are steadily improving and it's certainly a friendly place. There's fuel and a cafe on the circuit, but if the fare doesn't appeal or the fuel is either closed or over your credit card limit then there's also a cafe and petrol station at the entrance on the main road.

How To get There

Snetterton is between Thetford and Norwich on the A11. It's easy enough to find, because the A11 is essentially the only main road that leads to Norwich from anywhere. If your coming from the South then the circuit will be on your right, and is clearly signposted for both Snetterton Circuit and the Sunday market. If you're coming from the North then it's probably easiest to take the A47 from Kings Lynne and pick up the A11 just West of Norwich. In which case the circuit will be on your left.

Snetterton Circuit
Norwich, Norfolk NR16 2JU
Tel: +44 (0)1953 887303 Fax: +44 (0)1953 888220
http://www.motorsportvision.co.uk

Snetterton Circuit Notes

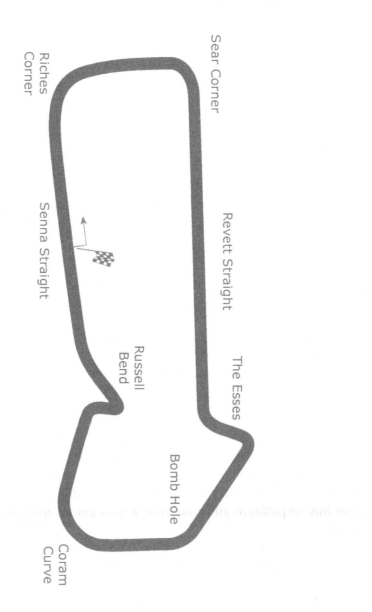

Thruxton

Thruxton circuit is near Andover, Hampshire. It sits on the very edge of Salisbury Plain, next to the A303, and surrounds a thriving general aviation airfield. All of which make the draconian and strictly enforced noise regulations just a little difficult to understand. There are very few trackdays of any sort here as a result. I once got black flagged for noise here on a BMW test day, riding a totally stock R1100S. The traffic on the dual carriageway was louder...

Anyway, if you get the chance to go you should. Thruxton is possibly the fastest circuit in the country. It's well surfaced and grippy, with enormous runoff areas in most places. It is also extremely bumpy and will favour a well set up bike. Err on the side of softness if you must muck about with your suspension, otherwise leave it on standard road settings until you have a reason not to. The surface is pretty hard on tyres as it seems to be rather abrasive.

On The Track

Leaving the pitlane (see illustration opposite) you come out onto a short leading straight into a fairly aggressive right/left/right chicane known as The Complex (Campbell, Cobb and Segrave). Getting your entry speed right here is critical, as over enthusiasm will see you running out of track on the way round. The right hand exit leads into a fast lefthander called Noble which suffers from one of the biggest problems with Thruxton. It's rather featureless which makes it easy to get a little lost on turn-ins and braking. After dispatching Noble, you essentially do the same going right through Goodwood, another featureless turn. Try to stay reasonably tight on the exit as you go into Church – probably the fastest bend anywhere in the UK. The line isn't important, but being smooth and, ultimately, brave is. Again it's quite bumpy, so be aware of that. It's quite steeply uphill which can help in bleeding off speed without braking if you need to, but despite any trepidation you may feel, if you get it right you will almost always be able to go faster than you think. Church leads into a long uphill drag which kinks gently before bursting into Club (the chicane). This is extremely tight though can be taken quite quickly. Watch out for highsides, which are very common here, and for being torpedoed by the nutter trying to get past you before the straight. If you need to take the pitlane, or indeed at the end of the session, you'll need to take a tight right at the end of the chicane. Otherwise, leave the Chicane on a fairly fast right hander, down the short start/finish straight, into Allard. Allard is a fast right hander with the pitlane exit on the right as you finish the corner. That's a lap.

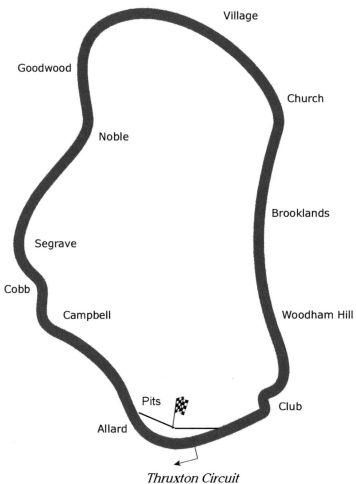

Thruxton Circuit

Facilities
There is fuel on the circuit and the nearest offsite petrol is about 5 miles down the A303 on the Andover exit.

How to Get There
When travelling to the circuit make sure that you're going to the right place – Thruxton village, just down the road, does not have any circuit access. Follow the brown 'Thruxton circuit' signs from the A303 which itself is accessed from Junction 8 on the M3 or by coming straight down the A34 from Oxford and beyond.

Thruxton Motorsport Centre
Andover, Hampshire SP11 8PW
Tel: 01264 882222 Fax: 01264 882201
http://www.thruxtonracing.co.uk

Thruxton Circuit: Notes

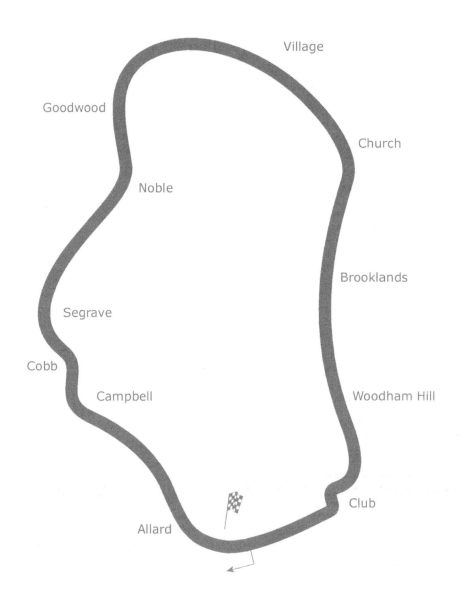

Checklists

Things to bring

Driving licence and joining instructions/disclaimer etc

One piece (or zip-up two piece) leathers

Waterproofs (optional)

Spare visor (maybe a dark one) optional

Cash/chequebook/card for petrol

Balance of fee for the day if required

Sense of humour!

Things to check on the bike

Chain tension and chain lube

Tyre pressure and wear

Brake pads, shoes and fluid level

Engine oil level and general condition of engine

Noise

Suspension settings and condition

General condition and track worthiness

If you are taking a trailer or van then also check you have your helmet, gloves, boots and bike keys with you!

Trackday companies

There is a huge number of companies offering trackdays, and the list is changing all the time as some start up and others stop. Obviously I can't claim experience of all of them, but here are a few that I have either ridden with myself or know people who have ridden with them. I have deliberately steered away from the real headbangers as that's not a place to go when you're starting out on the track. Or even if you're a veteran who wants to avoid getting involved in someone else's crash.

California Superbike School

If you decide that you really want to get into track riding seriously then this is really the only way to go. Track guru Keith Code set up the CSS specifically with you in mind. It's very much centred on racing and it is really training. You'll learn loads but it won't be as much fun as a regular trackday. Then again, you'll be faster and safer at the end of it...

Tel. 08700 671061 www.superbikeschool.co.uk

Focused Events

Another immensely professional outfit, with plenty of days throughout the UK and Europe. Genuinely geared to all levels of experience and very welcoming to novices, even offering financial incentives to first timers. Bike hire available.

Tel. 08702 646268. www.focusedevents.com

Hot Trax

Although they have groups at all levels, their inclusion of competition licence holders means that they may well be better suited to slightly more experienced track day goers. Extremely professional, though, and among the best for European visits if that's your bag.

Tel. 01908 566067. www.hottrax.co.uk

Motorcycle Folly

Originally set up as a way for a bunch of legal types to ride together on track, Motorcycle Folly is now one of the only not for profit trackday organisers left. Perhaps a tiny bit cliquey, they are still friendly, offer excellent value for money and are very novice friendly.

Tel. 07776 223734 www.motorcyclefolly.co.uk

No Limits

Also catering for all levels, No Limits have a good policy toward novices, with extra briefings on offer. Their European days are open pitlane, which should give an indication of their main market, though.

Tel. 01727 899173. www.nolimitstrackdays.com

Rapid Tracks

The track day arm of one of the best advanced riding schools in the country, Rapid Tracks is ideal for track day novices as well as seasoned veterans. A community spirit ensures good manners and there are plenty of instructors available. Recommended without reservation, though they never seem to have enough days available.

Tel 01296 630638 or   www.rapidtraining.co.uk

Further reading

There's just one book I can honestly say you will benefit from. Though it's a little dry in places and some of the explanations it contains will leave you scratching your head for a while, Keith Code's *A twist of the wrist* is *the* seminal work for anyone wanting to ride a motorbike faster. And when the bits that you puzzle over come together it all makes so much sense that you'll wonder why you didn't think of it before.